OUR CLASS, OUR VOICE

CREATING CHOICE AND AMPLIFYING AUTONOMY IN THE ELEMENTARY & MIDDLE SCHOOL CLASSROOM

GINA RUFFCORN

Special discounts are available on quantity purchases by schools, school districts, associations, and others. Email books@ daveburgessconsulting.com for pricing and details.

Published by Ditch That Textbook, whose printing operation is a division of Dave Burgess Consulting, Inc.
DitchThatTextbook.com
DaveBurgessConsulting.com

Cover design and interior design by Najdan Mancic, Iskon Design Inc.
Proofreading by Mairead Beeson

Library of Congress Control Number: 2022935624
Paperback ISBN: 978-1-956306-19-4
Ebook ISBN: 978-1-956306-20-0
First printing: April 2022

ENDORSEMENTS

I was in Gina's sixth-grade reading class. I remember the first time we walked into class Gina was standing there at the front of the class and greeted us as we walked in. Gina has done this for as long as I can remember. Even if she's grading papers, she will stop and look up to greet you in some welcoming manner, usually with a big, warm, "Hello Darling, how are ya?" You just felt welcome anytime you walked into the room and that feeling just made me, personally, want to be there full time.

Whenever there was a lesson to be taught to some rowdy fifth and sixth graders, you could leave it to Gina to find a way to keep those kids entertained. Gina just has that special personality that you can't help but be peppy and ready to tackle the day with some enthusiasm.

The next thing that stuck with me most about Gina is how caring she is about each one of her students. All these things I've mentioned prior pale in comparison to Gina's genuine care for your well-being. I will not lie. I am guilty of having called Gina mom in class before by accident, but that's further evidence of just how much she makes you feel welcome and like someone cares.

Gina was an overwhelming positive influence on every one. I can personally say that the things she taught me then and even now, have definitely shaped me into the man I am today.

—JADEN O.
Class of 2018, West Harrison CSD

I had Ms. Ruffcorn for two years, fifth and sixth grade. I loved when we were done reading *Hatchet* we made the posters of the stuff Brian was able to use to survive. I also loved reading and watching *The Outsiders*! I actually have a quote from the movie tattooed on my arm!

I was able to be myself in her classroom and we were always comfortable with her seating options! I feel like compared to other classrooms we were able to explore the things we enjoyed and she always made things fun. Ms. Ruffcorn also never took crap from anyone and I loved that. She will forever and always be one of my favorite teachers!

—**ALLISON H**
Class of 2018, West Harrison CSD

What didn't make Ms. Ruffcorn's class different?

Her classroom was always so inviting and warm and homey. Nothing about her room was plain or boring. She had little areas to read and relax, books everywhere, and fun decorations on every wall. Everything was colorful. We didn't use the harsh lights in a regular classroom all day long. Instead, she had the cutest lamps and lights to fill the room. Not to mention there was not a single regular boring, uncomfortable chair in her room.

I also loved that she incorporated Go Noodle and Skype into her classroom. I watched her students break into teams and Skype other classrooms around the world to guess where they were from using maps, coordinates, and all kinds of resources.

Her teaching techniques made kids love to learn and she pushed them to be the best version of themselves. Gina is a big part of my life and helped me grow into the person I am. I couldn't be more thankful to have had such an incredible teacher like her.

—**HAILEY A.**

Class of 2018 West Harrison CSD

As I thought about the difference between Ms. Ruffcorn's classroom and everyone else's. I thought, is that even a question to ask?

For everybody who just started fifth grade, it may not seem like that much of a difference, going from fifth to sixth grade, but it is a massive change. Every time I have a chance for a class in her room, I'm extremely happy. The way Ms. Ruffcorn brings fun and games into learning is incredible. It's not as silent and serious as my other classes. The room has a genuine child-like feeling. Like no matter how old or mature you are, it will always, and I mean always, bring out the child in you.

So to sum up my answer, Ms. Ruffcorn's room is a place you can go to if you feel stressed or pressured no matter what grade.

—**SHAWN F.**

Class of 2025, West Harrison CSD

Gina contacted me and asked me to describe what made not only her, but her classroom, different from my other teachers' throughout my school experience. The truth is, there is no comparison between her and other teachers because Gina is a one-of-a-kind woman. She'll leave an impact that will last a lifetime on every single student she interacts with.

She is the type of woman that every parent hopes their kid will someday become. Someone that you can always depend on, no matter the time of day or the situation at hand.

Gina made her classroom feel like home, a room you could walk into and you were greeted with a warm smile and welcoming hug. A judgment free zone. A carefree place where the rest of the world's problems could not touch. A safe space. Many of us needed that at a young age. The weight of the world simply dropped off your shoulders when you walked in the door.

Gina will always hold a special place in my heart, simply for the fact that she was more like family than just a teacher to me. Even now, in my adult life with work and raising kids, Gina still takes the time out of her busy schedule to check in on me. The amount of love, kindness and passion for teaching that Gina holds is unmatched by any teacher I've ever seen.

—**SHELBY L.**
Class of 2018, West Harrison CSD

The way to describe Ms. Gina Ruffcorn's room isn't with words. Experiencing the positivity, style, and teachings in that room will be sure to leave one speechless. She sets up her room not as a traditional classroom but in a way where people of all walks of life can feel accepted, heard, or even just present. She makes anyone feel accomplished and valuable with every obstacle that may come his/her way.

The room itself was filled with colors, scents, decorations, music, laughter, and fun. Walking into that room, one can just feel that the energy of the space shifts so stress and negativity are not promoted. The seats are not a regular desk and chair; no, they are fitness balls, cushions, bean bags.

It felt as if that room could withstand every crazy idea, every off-the-wall plan, any dance party, and especially the wind-down time. Although students love to get up and have fun, there were still many times when we would sit to read an empowering novel. Everyone had a role in that room. Not one person was ever excluded from the incredible lessons Ms. Gina Ruffcorn had to share.

—**RILEY A.**

Class of 2023, West Harrison CSD

This collection of experiences and ideas is lovingly dedicated to each and every one of the students who left a lasting impression with me. Listening to and learning from all of you shaped me into the teacher that I would have wanted when I was a student.

TABLE OF CONTENTS

FOREWORD

I vividly remember one of my first in-person conversations with Gina Ruffcorn, which took place as we meandered through the late-afternoon streets of downtown Austin. We had attended several presentations earlier in the day at the Texas Computer Education Association Conference. The sessions focused on using technology to empower students and virtually connect classrooms. Gina spoke passionately about her teaching philosophy and the student agency she had successfully fostered as we walked. In contrast to some of the day's presenters, her methods were easy to understand and grounded in techniques that she had honed in her classroom. I recommended that she write a book.

That conversation took place in February 2015. Since then, Gina and her students have continued to teach me and countless others new ways of developing a class culture centered on student autonomy. On many occasions, her students have virtually connected with groups of educators I was training around the globe—from Kenya to California. Gina didn't have to say much on those calls; her students took the lead and explained how their classroom operated and why her methods helped them succeed. On one occasion, Gina had to miss school on a day her students were supposed to connect with a group of educators. Instead of canceling our call, she allowed her students to run the session without her. They owned the opportunity. The teachers in my session left both impressed and inspired to give their own students more voice and choice.

Gina has also profoundly impacted my own career as a teacher and an author. When we first started collaborating over a decade ago, we had a lot in common. We both taught in rural, culturally isolated areas. We were both fifth-grade teachers. We were both looking to emerging technologies to help our students see the incredible possibilities, diverse perspectives, and inspiring people outside our small towns. Our work together as we tried to meet the challenges in our local communities helped me develop many of the techniques and projects that led to my recognition as a Global Teacher Prize finalist and Pennsylvania Teacher of the Year. As I've written in my books about how a healthy democratic society relies on student agency in schools, I've often pictured Gina's students as examples of how we can get education right.

I could not be more excited about this book. Selfishly, I am eager to incorporate new classroom practices based on tips found in the following chapters. More importantly, I am thrilled that others will finally be able to benefit from the expertise of one of the most authentic and excellent teachers I've met anywhere in the world. Our children will inherit this planet from us sooner than we realize. The practical ideas in this book are a way to ensure they are prepared to shape it into something extraordinary.

—**MICHAEL SOSKIL**

Pennsylvania Teacher of the Year

Global Teacher Prize Top Ten Finalist

INTRODUCTION

Making decisions in daily life is a fundamental human need. As adults, the ability to make our own decisions motivates us to create, shape, and meaningfully contribute to our own choices. It connects us. It gives us purpose.

Students crave those same feelings.

As an undergrad, I don't remember any of my pre-service coursework ever mentioning student choice or autonomy. The prevailing focus was on the teacher, the classroom management, and the presentation of the content material. No one ever addressed the students' thoughts. Their opinions. Their choices. Their need for autonomy.

I had some epic power struggles with students in my first years of teaching, many of which could have been completely avoided. What if the classroom's culture could have been improved by talking to the kids and getting their input? Think about that. What if the kids felt like they were a part of the decision-making process in their day?

What if your chair-tipping student could benefit from alternative seating? No more reminders or escalated voices insistently nagging about all four legs needing to be on the floor. Seating choices completely change the entire situation.

How about that time after recess when no one can get settled back down? Would the kids respond more calmly to the lights being dimmed while they worked, or if they listened to a read-aloud? Students are capable of making decisions and choosing the setting that works best for them.

Simply surviving in a classroom from day to day should not be a goal for you or for the students. Ask yourself how you could alter your daily classroom reality by giving the students choices and making small adjustments based on simple decisions. How would the classroom environment thrive if the students could make choices and decisions that benefitted them?

Honor your students' voices and build the classroom with them. It has unimaginable benefits.

Honor your students' voices and build the classroom with them. It has unimaginable benefits. Asking their opinions, giving them a say in daily operations, or allowing them to vote on an activity makes students feel important and valued. My classroom was built—and continues to flourish—based on the ideas and experiences on each page.

Take your students into account when you're making plans for the classroom—from creating your physical space to operating it on a daily basis. I am certain of that fact because eighteen years later, I have tried, revised, and successfully implemented every idea in this book with my own students in my own classroom.

Creating choices and opportunities for student autonomy is the foundation for this book's three areas of concentration: Providing Choices, Creating a Classroom, and Establishing

Relationships. In this book, I share ideas directly from my own fifth-grade room. Of course, just because I teach fifth grade doesn't mean you do. But the tips, suggestions, and strategies in this book apply to all different ages in the elementary and middle school world, even into the high school realm.

In this book, you'll also hear from my students. They'll tell you in their own voices why certain decisions worked for them. You'll also hear from Isabelle Foland, who was one of my fifth graders years ago. As of the publication of this book, Isabelle is planning to major in journalism and mass communication at the University of Iowa.

"What I remember most from her class was feeling like there were almost no limits on my creativity," Isabelle said. "The way she teaches encourages kids to have freedom and independence while also teaching them to make better choices. I would say Ms. Ruffcorn has a reputation within our school for her unique yet effective and fun teaching style. I was very eager to find out exactly how her methods came to be."

So, what did I ask the journalist to do? Interview me! You'll find parts of my interview with Isabelle throughout the book.

As you read this book, I encourage you to make the modifications to fit your situation, which might look different for kindergarten, middle school, and high school classes. I invite you to examine each idea and truly seek out how you might use it or adapt it to give your students more autonomy and voice. That's the goal here—the students and their needs to feel seen, heard, and known.

A few years ago, my school district was interviewing administrator candidates. One contender stopped outside our classroom with the current administrator. "Here is our fifth grade," our administrator said. "You may not agree with her methods, but you can't argue with her results."

I took the comment as a compliment. Many of my methods may not be things that everyone would agree with. I'm okay with that. My methods work for me and for my students. We're the ones living in room 508. It's our home.

How do we determine the best methods for us—even if they're common, traditional approaches—to get the results we seek?

Ask yourself what you're open to trying. What are you really, truly open to trying? Decide what you want your classroom to look like—with your students.

Pick and choose the concepts that speak to you.

Then think about your students.

Ask yourself:

Which traditional methods can I revise?

How would they improve my students' experiences in my classroom?

How would they give the students choice and autonomy?

PROVIDING CHOICES

Inherently all people need to feel like they matter. Everyone wants to be noticed, to be seen, to be valued for their thoughts and abilities. Kids in classrooms are no different.

This section explores many ideas focused on the central theme of offering student choices that can be used or adapted for any classroom.

As you read, think about you, your teaching style, your grade level, your classroom, and your students.

Ask yourself:

What could my version of student choice look like?

CHAPTER ONE

Gathering Student Input

The changes that I have made to my daily routines, my classroom management style, and my learning environment are based on the most important factors present in the classroom: the kids.

I know: that doesn't sound like a startling revelation. Hear me out.

I have changed my class. My decisions are not made because of the students. They are made *with* the students. No one ever seems to suggest asking the kids' opinions about the classroom operations. It doesn't make sense to me. Teachers' choices affect the kids directly, every minute, all day

My decisions are not made because of the students. They are made with the students.

long. However, no one ever seems to give them an opportunity to consistently make their voices heard. The students' lack of choice seems odd to me.

What if a student identified something to help the classroom run more efficiently? What if they saw an adjustment that could help everyone feel happier or be more successful? Shouldn't that student get the opportunity to make a suggestion?

Do you suppose they feel like no one cares about their needs? Do they think things are being done "to them" instead of "with them"? Do the kids feel that their voices aren't important to you and in their classroom? And when they feel that way, how does that impact their learning and growth?

Those are the kinds of wonders that I ruminate about. The more I put myself in the kids' shoes, the more I thought I needed to change. The kids who share the space with me ought to have input into its operations.

Taking those thoughts into account, I questioned my past classroom management decisions.

- ► Had I made things harder on myself and the students by not considering these ideas earlier?
- ► Would there have been fewer issues or less stress if I had talked to the kids and made some mutually agreed upon changes?
- ► Were there things I had never considered before because I wasn't a student in my classroom?
- ► Should classroom management be a two-way street?
- ► Should the students have more choices and decision-making options?

I needed to know what my students wanted in a classroom in order to be more productive learners. That is the 'why' behind the creation of student surveys.

FIRST-WEEK STUDENT SURVEY

When I begin the year, my new students complete a survey. It's not a learner inventory. It's not a "tell me about your summer" writing piece. It's a survey of them as students.

QUESTIONS FOR FIRST-WEEK SURVEYS

- What is your favorite thing about school? Why?
- What do you dislike the most about school? Why?
- How do you like to learn?
- What works best for you?
- What are you looking forward to the most in fifth grade?
- What are you most worried about as fifth grade begins?
- What is something you want me to know about you?
- What do you know about your teacher?
- What do you expect or want from your teacher?

The results of those initial questions help me begin to shape our year together. We can build on many of the kids' favorite things about school. Hard dislikes can be altered or discontinued, if possible. For instance, if the group dislikes one online practice site over another, that's an easy concession to make.

If group work or partner activities are favorites, I begin to plan opportunities for collaboration.

I talk at length about the things from the survey that they anticipate most. We do a wide variety of unique activities during the year. I like to make a big deal out of those examples to build interest and engagement. I share information about virtual field trips, mystery location sessions, and other cool things that make our year special. By the time I am done chatting up all of the experiences we will have together, the kids' eyes are shining, and they're raring to begin.

The worries from the survey are often not shared aloud. We will, however, address common concerns that quite a few of the incoming students shared. Oftentimes, the worries are easily dispelled. Homework-related fears are the most common. Getting those thoughts out of the way noticeably changes the atmosphere in the room. The relief is almost palpable. Offering reassurance about the scary things instantly builds connections to the kids.

I want to know as much about the students as individuals as possible. That's the focus of the "What do you want me to know about you?" question. I've learned some really interesting information over the years. Sometimes kids will try to offer up phrases they have heard their parents say about learning difficulties from previous school years. They'll say, "I can't memorize math facts because I have short-term memory loss disease," or "I need more one-on-one time in math because my mom wasn't good at math either." Other times, children use this question to explain what they want to do when they grow up. Some responses are truly one of a kind. One is pretty much cemented in my memory: "I like to read horror books. I believe in ghosts, and I want to learn more about witchcraft so I can practice magic and spells and speak with the dead and stuff." Kids will share all sorts of revelations if you ask.

Dispelling or clarifying things that kids think they know about me helps build connections with them. It also gives me a chance to explain the 'why' behind some aspects of classroom management style. For example, a student's answer was, "I know it's gonna be an easy year. We never have to do homework cuz my brother's friend said so." In that case, the student did not know as much as he thought he did. Once I tackled his misconception, the whole class understood that if they got their work done in class, *then* there wasn't any homework. The older brother's friend was wrong, and the rumor was quieted.

The feedback from the last question—"What do you expect or want from your teacher?"—never gives me much information. But it serves a greater purpose. It lets the students know that they can have expectations of me as their teacher. The idea of telling a teacher what they want or expect from them is an unfamiliar experience for students. The question sets the stage for them to begin to understand that, as the year unfolds, I will aspire to rise to their expectations of me.

The survey is an incredibly valuable tool. The way I relate to students, the activities I decide to include in lessons, and the pitfalls I need to avoid are all examples of ways the students' voices help inform the way I teach. Without the guidance from their replies, I'd be stuck floundering until I accidentally tripped across things that worked, or worse yet, I'd fall face-first into a situation I could have avoided. Each year I've used the questionnaire, I've gained useful insights that shape the way I interact with my students.

PULSE CHECKS
(NO MEDICAL TRAINING REQUIRED)

I pose prompts to gauge students' thoughts and opinions once every nine weeks, which I call 'pulse checks'. Pulse checks are informal surveys where I ask these simple questions:

- ► What are three things we need more of in our classroom?
- ► What are three things we need less of or to get rid of?
- ► What do you wish the teacher knew?

Those three questions are the bedrock of the quarterly pulse checks. I've added extra ones at times, but I don't want the pulse checks to become overwhelming essays. I want the students to legitimately reflect on our experiences. After all, I don't know what I don't know. It's another chance to share their unique voice.

I've given the kids the option to answer anonymously if that makes the responses more honest. Let me issue a word of caution here: If you don't want unflinchingly candid responses, do not ask kids for their opinions. You can't get angry or bent out of shape based on their observations. It's important to make sure that you are open and ready to accept or honor the kids' thoughts. Pulse checks are only valid if you genuinely want to understand the students' perspectives.

The kids turn their pulse checks face-down, and I collect and review them before the next school day. The following morning, during our daily overview, the Secretary goes to the board with the Insurance Officer. (These are two classroom jobs you'll learn more about in Chapter 3.) Each is in charge of recording the answers in two columns: "things that we need more of" and "things we need less of." I read the suggestions while the kids record them on the board. Once all of the responses are recorded, we discuss them as a large group.

Student feedback can lead to many adjustments. Generally, their proposals are simple requests. Coming to a common consensus on ways to change our routines requires flexibility on everyone's part. When students lead the discussion about their opinions, it builds a sense of community in the classroom.

The suggestions students make are usually in their best interest. After all, that's why they chose those changes. Personally, I don't ever remember them suggesting anything that didn't benefit me in some way.

That being said, I've never had a class of students purposely attempting to weasel out of work or get away with absurd requests. The kids seem to genuinely understand the purpose of the pulse check. Kids usually don't take the offer for granted or make a mockery of it. Truly, they want to have a say in the decisions that affect them daily.

Here's a taste of what kids usually want:

- More game-type learning activities
- Different classroom coupon options
- More escape rooms
- More time to work on assignments (like a study hall)
- Four GoNoodles in the morning instead of just three

► More partnering for activities or projects

► Extra time added to independent reading period

Some items are non-negotiable. For example, as much as they don't like practice problems in math, getting rid of them completely isn't a possibility. I can lessen the number of problems or vary the way we practice in class, but I can't discontinue practice problems entirely. Another frequent request is an increase in P.E. classes. I have no control over how many days per week the class has P.E. I understand they want more P.E. days, but that is an administrative decision. If I can't accommodate the students' suggestions or if they are administrative in nature, I explain that.

There's incredible benefit to talking about impossible requests and clarifying my decisions.

There's incredible benefit to talking about impossible requests and clarifying my decisions. Students feel like their concerns have at least been heard and valued. If they understand the situation, they are more likely to accept certain rules and regulations that they had taken issue with before.

The list of things students have responded that we need less of has included:

► Math videos

► Typing practice

► Online spelling word practice

► Read-aloud time

► Math time

There are even times when the students' answers mirror my thoughts on what we need less of. For example, "people talking when they shouldn't be." The fact that a majority of the class wanted the same thing that I did was powerful. Their peers were annoyed with the behavior as well. It's powerful to be able to say that your neighbors and your teacher all agree that talking excessively is distracting. Students can remind blurters and chatters that it's not just the teacher that needs them to stop. The fact that their classmates also want them to quit interrupting our learning is a strong deterrent.

The "What do you wish the teacher knew?" question is important. It lets the students privately share concerns. Sometimes, this is easier to do in writing, especially if it's an issue they are embarrassed about or can't bring themselves to vocalize.

In a very small class of thirteen students, I had a learner who struggled in math. She didn't want everyone to know how hard it was for her. She got anxious; She wouldn't ask for help, she didn't even raise her hand to have me scoot over to help her. She knew she needed help, but she didn't know how to get it without everyone seeing her struggle.

When she shared this with me during a pulse check, we came up with a secret cue system. When she needed help, she flagged me in a way no one noticed, and I made my way over to her inconspicuously. I checked on others and then on her. That way, it didn't seem like she was the only person I was assisting. It worked for her, and she felt less self-conscious. If she hadn't shared her concerns, I couldn't have supported her needs.

SPECIALIZED SURVEY SITUATIONS

Sometimes, a consistent issue I can't figure out impacts the class. Sometimes, negative behaviors hurt our classroom community. That's when I pop in a specialized student survey. These situations don't happen often, but when they do, it's essential to get the students' thoughts and opinions.

One time, a group of boys was being disrespectful outside of our classroom. One day in particular, several of them had been rude in the lunchroom and on the way back from lunch. Those same boys were written up at recess for breaking the rules and thrown out of Art class. The other students were upset because they were missing out on things and getting chastised for the behavior of a few kids. The rest of the class was consistently distressed about the situation. Many of the kids would return to the classroom, adamantly stressing their innocence during situations. They were concerned about losing privileges or rewards based on other students' bad decisions. Obviously, there was a significant need to collect some student feedback regarding the concept of respect with a specialized survey.

Since the issue seemed to be specifically isolated to just a few kids, those were the only survey participants. The feedback from the questions showed their honest insights—or lack thereof. Using their responses, I developed a mini respect unit for the group. I grounded the group from all Art, P.E., and music classes while we worked our way through the issues. As we discussed the disrespectful behavior and explored why it was happening, I used the answers from the survey to drive the conversations. As a group, we talked about how to be respectful and what to do in different situations in order to not show disrespect to others. After a few weeks, we had formulated a few workable solutions that would demonstrate respect to ourselves and to others.

The survey responses helped me to understand their perspectives and allowed me to work collaboratively with the boys on a solution.

SURVEYS BOOST CLASSROOM COMMUNITY

Taking informal surveys in my classroom has made classroom management a two-way street. They create immeasurable differences in the way our classroom operates. Our surveys allow student voices to be heard and honored. Students have more ownership of the classroom environment and what we do in it. When we openly acknowledge the suggestions and comments the kids make, it improves the tone of the classroom culture.

Student surveys have shown me so much about my kids' wants and needs. We can easily make most of their suggested changes to make our classroom match their vision. I'm open to their input. When they know their teacher really listens to them, it builds a stronger relationship with the students. Being flexible and open to change are life skills that kids will need as they continue throughout their school years and beyond. Our surveys—and how we use the input gathered through them—show students how that should look.

CHAPTER TWO

Voting

What's important to the students in a classroom? Do we know?

Do we ever ask them?

Shouldn't we?

I've mulled over all of those questions. When I thought back to my teaching classes, I was certain that none of my instructors ever suggested that we ask the kids their opinions about classroom decisions. To me, the concept made perfect sense. It was almost a no-brainer. If the kids were the ones being affected by my management ideas, then why had I never consulted them?

If the kids were the ones being affected by my management ideas, then why had I never consulted them?

Perhaps it was my overinflated ego: *This is my classroom, and, therefore, my rules are my rules.*

They're kids. They do what they're told to do.

Maybe I was scared of losing control of the situation? *What if chaos broke out?* I thought. *Would I be able to establish order ever again?*

Small choices that seem insignificant to adults are a big deal for kids.

Would it make me weak? Would the kids think I didn't know what I was doing?

Would I lose their respect?

Would they run all over me?

There were suddenly a ton of uncomfortable, awkward notions rolling around in my head.

I knew that I reacted better in situations where I thought my ideas and opinions were being taken into account. It made sense that the same premise would hold true for students.

EVERY STUDENT GETS A VOTE: MAJORITY RULES

It shouldn't be up to me to make all of the class' decisions. And honestly, I get tired of deciding things. There's some outrageous quote that I read once that estimated the amount of decisions teachers make every day. It was exhausting just looking at the number. At the end of a school day, I don't want to decide anything, not even what's for supper. That's why I let students vote.

Oftentimes, kids don't really get the opportunity to make many decisions. They need practice. Every time they get to decide on anything that directly affects them, they feel powerful. Small choices that seem insignificant to adults are a big deal for kids. That's also how children learn to make bigger, more important decisions: by starting with the little ones. Building a sense of ownership for their choices is empowering for kids. By honoring them as individuals, they have a voice in the classroom.

My class votes on all sorts of non-essential items. It allows the kids to feel like their beliefs are honored. They have a say in things because they have a vested interest in the way the classroom runs. All votes are counted fairly by the student who is our Official Counter (another classroom job you'll learn about in the next chapter). Democracy rules.

EXAMPLES OF THINGS WE VOTE ON:

♥ Classroom lighting
  * Sometimes we work with the overhead classroom lights on. Other times, we turn them off and use lamps placed around the room.

♥ Order of our morning content areas
  * We have a literacy block first thing in the morning. I share my plans for reading and spelling with the kids. It makes no difference to me which one I teach first, so they get to decide. Both content areas are covered, but letting the kids choose which one comes first makes a huge difference in their attitudes as we begin.

♥ Classroom decorations for holidays and seasons

* Kids rarely get to decorate entirely on their own. The first time I bring seasonal boxes into the room, students are unclear about where things are "supposed to go." I explain that it's up to them, that they should figure out how they want the room to look. Not being told what to do all of the time is a new concept for many students. Being able to choose where the decorations go gives them ownership of the way the room looks. Then, when the decorations are up, they all care for them because they're the ones who chose them and decorated the room. That's the buy-in for them.

* Students often refer back to the memories of decorating the classroom as one of their favorite things on the end-of-the-year survey. "When we got to do the Christmas lights together was one of my most memorable moments this year." Hunter

♥ Class arrangements for skills practice

* Sometimes we do whole-class practice. Other times, we practice individually. When it doesn't make a difference to me, the students choose.

♥ Partners for activities

* Sometimes students pick their own partners. Other times, they choose to pull sticks to select partners randomly.

♥ Read-aloud literature genre
* The students pick the type of novel and then the specific book we listen to for reading-aloud.

♥ The type of project for an assignment
* Having the freedom to vote on the type of project that kids get to submit for an assignment increases creativity. Offering variety for project creation lets students rely on their strengths as they show you what they learned. I give them a few options to start with so they don't become overwhelmed. Once, during novel studies in reading, one student chose to create a game board using the plot from the story. Another chose to illustrate a 'wanted poster' for the two main characters in her novel. Someone else modeled a diorama of the novel's setting.

The list could go on forever. Perhaps the greatest thing about student voting is there is no arguing or grouching afterward. They all voted, and it was their decision. The Official Counter counted their raised hands. All unanimous decisions are final.

Based on consistent student feedback, they're huge advocates of voting, and, based on my experience, it has many positive impacts for students of all ages. Understanding that their voice matters is empowering for kids. Fairness is also a huge concept for students. Taking part in activities that reinforce fairness helps kids learn how most decisions are made. Making a choice and casting a vote, then accepting the outcome gracefully is a necessary life skill that makes my kids better citizens of our district.

I asked my kids: "What was one of the best things about fifth grade?"

Sage's answer:

> Being able to vote if want to read books or do a project.

Hannah's opinion:

> I like to vote on lots of things.

SUPER SECRET SQUIRREL VOTING

Sometimes, anonymous voting is necessary. Sometimes, someone's feelings could be hurt by the outcome. For example, when we vote on "pick your own partner or let the sticks pick," some students know that they don't want to choose their recess buddy. That person may be great to play tag or kickball with, but they aren't a productive partner. There's no need to hurt anyone's feelings by openly casting a vote against picking their own partners.

For those special circumstances, we use something that I call "Super Secret Squirrel" voting.

(Of course, if your students are older and the term "Super Secret Squirrel" voting wouldn't work with them, you can always just call it anonymous voting!) Everyone grabs a scrap of paper and casts a vote. I read the votes, and the Official Counter tallies the results on the board. No feelings are hurt, and the decision stands.

"Super Secret Squirrel" voting is also used when we need to vote on special items or awards. At the end of the school year, the elementary school holds an awards assembly. Each teacher nominates a student for various awards: leadership, growth mindset, best teammate, kindest, and best attitude awards. The decision

WHY IS IT CALLED "SUPER SECRET SQUIRREL" VOTING?

There are unique times when there needs to be a way to separate a routine voting situation from a more personal decision type of vote. Secret voting requires a secret-sounding name. That name became Super Secret Squirrel. I love alliteration, and squirrels do secretly hide things they don't want other animals to find out about. During Super Secret Squirrel voting, the kids 'squirrel away' and write their vote privately, then immediately hide it from others and bring it directly to me. It's a silly name that the kids and I get a kick out of saying. Watching their squirrel behaviors to keep their votes secret is hilarious!

shouldn't be up to just me, so I include my students in the voting process. A "Super Secret Squirrel" vote is imperative in that kind of situation. All votes come to me, and no one ever needs to know who voted for whom. Everyone gets a chance to honestly select the person they believe should win.

VOTING GIVES EVERY STUDENT AN EQUAL VOICE

Whole-class voting further reinforces the concept of honoring the kids' decisions. Their opinions have power. Having everyone cast a vote eliminates the tired, old "teacher's favorite" theory. My vote carries the exact same weight as a student's vote. There's no rumbling about favoritism when the winner is announced. Letting the students' votes decide the outcome also circumvents the possibility of the award going to someone who "knows how to put on a good show." There are always those kids who are polite, kind, personable, and mannerly in front of adults but capable of being rude, snotty, and mean when we're not looking. Kids know best which classmate is genuine. Being selected by your peers is a positive, meaningful experience for the kids who are chosen. Oftentimes, the students' votes are surprising. I know the kids from a teacher's perspective; they know each other very differently. I honestly believe their selections are way more conscientious than mine.

ISABELLE: Why did you choose to begin your teaching career at West Harrison in small-town Iowa of all places?

GINA: I student-taught in this building across the hall from the room I teach in now. Shortly after I graduated, the district posted a position for an 'outreach' teacher. The job that I applied for hadn't existed before. It didn't have a name, and it had no real guidelines. As the superintendent pitched the idea, I thought it sounded interesting. It sounded challenging and kinda cool. The concept of being able to go out and reach those kids that weren't having any luck in a normal, traditional setting appealed to me.

CHAPTER THREE

Classroom Jobs and Committees

B efore I found my forever home as a fifth-grade teacher, I taught first grade. When I happily moved to the upper elementary, I put away many items—and many strategies—I used with my littles, never thinking I would need them again. In fifth grade, I discovered that I seemed to be spending a ton of time on the small operational tasks of running a classroom. Flyers didn't get mailed home because I got busy and over-looked them. The room was messy. I was hardly ever on time transitioning from subject to subject because I couldn't see the clock. It was exhausting. I was constantly scrambling, and managing the classroom minutia made me a hot mess. Then I remembered classroom jobs from my time with the littles!

The teacher shouldn't be the only one to make the room run smoothly. Students can take on those responsibilities by taking on classroom jobs and serving in classroom committees.

JOBS FOR UPPER ELEMENTARY STUDENTS?

I'd never seen any fifth-grade classrooms where the students had jobs. I didn't think I had ever even heard classroom jobs mentioned in an upper elementary room, but I wasn't sure why. It didn't make much sense to give jobs to lower elementary students and then discard the concept when they were older. After all, lower elementary kids were really too young to do much to genuinely provide help. Plus, there were a bunch of them and only one of me.

What could my kids do to make the room run better?

I investigated but didn't find many examples of classroom jobs for older kids. So I dug through my stored resources from my littles, kept some ideas, and then added my own. What could my kids do to make the room run better? What shouldn't they be allowed to do? I devised a list of classroom jobs that would "employ" my students. Over time, I have added, subtracted, and honed the classroom job list. This is the one currently in use in my room.

MS. RUFFCORN'S CLASSROOM JOBS LIST

- ❧ DISTRIBUTOR: Returns all papers or supplies to students
- ❧ RECYCLER: Ensures all paper products get put in the recycle bin and empties the bin when necessary
- ❧ MAIL CARRIER: Puts mail, notes, and fliers into student mailboxes
- ❧ SECRETARY: Writes the day's agenda on the board, announces the daily schedule and lunch menu, maintains the classroom calendar, and adds activities to the calendar as necessary
- ❧ STICK PULLER: Pulls sticks to choose student names for activities
- ❧ BOARD MONITOR: Maintains and wipes off whiteboards as necessary
- ❧ MESSENGER: Runs all errands outside of the classroom
- ❧ LIBRARIANS: Maintains the classroom library and separates books by genre and author's last name (requires two students due to the size of the library)
- ❧ ELECTRICIAN: Turns on and off all classroom lights, operates the projector for the monitor, and cares for any seasonal lights
- ❧ TABLE CHECKER: Checks tables and surrounding areas for scraps, schnibbles, and clutter before releasing students to leave the room

♥ SUPPLIER: Monitors and straightens the classroom supply area and lets the teacher know if supplies are needed

♥ ATTENDANCE MONITOR: Collects missing assignments for students who are absent, explains them, and helps with notes for their return

♥ TIME KEEPER: Supervises the time schedule, watches the clock, and keeps the class accurately on task

♥ RECESS HELPER: Brings forgotten equipment, jackets, etc., back inside the classroom, accompanies injured children to the nurse, gathers people to help hold the doors on the way back inside

♥ LINE LEADER: Leads and monitors the line when the class leaves the room

♥ INSURANCE OFFICER: Assists students who spill or drop items, assists with small classroom accidents (i.e., rubber cement spills, water spills, etc.), and ensures that the hallway is clean and lockers are closed at the end of the day

♥ GONOODLER: Chooses the GoNoodle activities for the entire week

♥ CABINET & CRATE CAPTAIN: Straightens the board and card game cabinet after indoor recess and after Friday morning unplugged time, also checks the cleanliness of everyone's crates on Monday mornings

♥ OFFICIAL COUNTER: Counts and tallies responses to votes

♥ DOOR HOLDER: Holds the second spot in line and is in charge of all door holding

WHAT ARE "SCHNIBBLES?" IS THAT A REAL WORD?

Yes! Schnibbles is actually a real word, a far more common term for "scraps," or "small pieces," in parts of the United States that were largely settled by German immigrants. The term comes from German schnippel, meaning "scraps." The Table Checker becomes very familiar with schnibbles.

MANAGING CLASSROOM JOBS

Implementing classroom jobs must be done with complete seriousness and fidelity to truly make a difference in the classroom. For jobs to be meaningful to students, the tasks must be genuine. There will be times when, for instance, the Official Counter is slower than frozen syrup at getting hands counted when your class is voting. Or your Time Keeper is daydreaming, so now the class is late for a special. At those times, you will think, "Why don't I just do this stuff myself?" or "What difference will it make if I just do the job for the Frozen-Syrup-Official-Counter so we can move on?" Resist the urge to overrun the jobs and devalue the tasks being performed by the kids. They chose the jobs they are doing. Allow them the autonomy to do them well.

I introduce jobs and their requirements in the first week of school. I make a huge deal out of the importance of everyone sharing the work of running our classroom. I display the job titles on the only bulletin board in my room. The kids decorate wooden clothespins with their names, and we pull popsicle sticks to ensure that job picking is as fair as possible. When a student's name is pulled on a popsicle stick, that student gets to choose a job from the job board. That way, they pick the job they want to do. Sometimes, students will have the same job for multiple weeks. They clip their clothespin to the tag associated with the job they choose. We change jobs every week unless it's a short school week. If the week isn't a full five days, we vote to decide whether or not we change jobs or hold on to the ones they currently have.

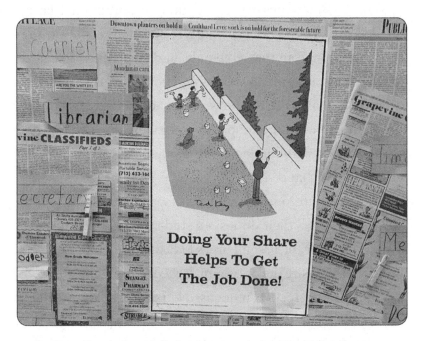

Students clip cards with their jobs using clothespins with their names.

The students take their job responsibilities more seriously as time passes, and they realize how much we rely on them for the classroom to run smoothly. Some jobs are highly sought after. It's interesting to watch the kids try different jobs or gravitate to those that are suited to their personalities and skills. Secretaries are generally some of the more self-confident kids; they enjoy being in front of the class to start our day and share information we all need to know. Usually, the Secretaries also have really great handwriting. Kids who thrive on structure and like to be in charge want to be the Time Keeper. Board Monitor and Cabinet Captain jobs seem more appealing to introverted kids who aren't yet comfortable with the focus being on them.

The first few weeks of jobs are purely adventures in trial and error as the kids pick jobs. I'll answer questions about the job's responsibilities, but that's the only guidance I offer. I've never had students ask me which job they should choose. It's not my decision to make. I've also never heard the kids ask each other about which jobs they should pick. Usually, they won't share which they're planning on picking, so no one takes it before they get their chance.

Since they are kids, every once in a while, someone drops the ball and neglects their duties. As students see each other performing in their roles, sometimes kids who aren't well suited to certain tasks desire the prestige attached to a certain job. So, for example, the overactive, unfocused kid chooses Time Keeper, a job that depends on attention. Sometimes stepping out of their comfort zone and trying something new is positive and can be a real confidence booster, but not always. If the tasks aren't being attended to properly, the student gets a couple of reminders. If things still don't improve, then the Insurance Officer is asked to step in and take over. The well-meaning Time Keeper then goes "on vacation" for the rest of the week. Getting reassigned isn't an experience that takes place very often. Having to remove your clip and relinquish your job to the classroom Insurance Officer is a rare occurrence. Holding each other accountable is something my kids are adamant about. They take great personal pride in doing their jobs.

One year, I had a class that was predominantly female. They were my alpha females. They chose all the jobs that called for time management, organization, and being in charge. However, no matter how much they all wanted to be Secretary, not one of them was ever successful in securing the position. They were thwarted by a savvy boy who loved to announce our morning information, boasted amazing handwriting, and had a knack for overseeing things perfectly. Eventually, they all gave up and carried out the other jobs while the boy with the amazing penmanship was Secretary all year. The moral of the story is that classroom jobs are genuine opportunities for students to make a choice free from bias and based only on the students' personal strengths and abilities.

JOBS MAKE THE CLASS FLOW

I fully depend on the students to perform the tasks required by the job they have chosen. The jobs are a vital, necessary part of our classroom environment. I do my job, and they do theirs; that's how we keep everything working efficiently. The feedback I've collected over time has confirmed my decision to implement jobs for my classroom:

"Jobs make me feel like I am involved in the class." Brady

"I think a classroom needs to have jobs so all the kids will have responsibilities." Maggie

"Having jobs makes me feel like I'm really helping the classroom." Mason

"Kids should always get to choose our own jobs." Parker

Allowing my kids to take over areas of our classroom operations has given them a sense of purpose. Students get some control over their environment as they perform their duties for the week. Jobs give them a sense of belonging to our room.

CLASSROOM COMMITTEES

In the real world, we adults aren't assigned our jobs by pulling popsicle sticks. We didn't become educators because someone randomly chose the profession for us. We had a passion for it. We had already developed some of the prerequisite skills. Some of us might say we were born educators. We studied and worked to hone our craft.

Acknowledging students' abilities and interests further increases their feeling of belonging.

It's the same way with my students. Our classroom committees honor some prerequisite

skills that students bring in the door from day one. Acknowledging those abilities and interests further increases their feeling of belonging. Committees also help students acclimate to an environment they'll see in the work world. Many organizations form project groups like these to complete certain duties and responsibilities. When our classroom committees mimic these groups, they foster teamwork and collaboration amongst the students. They also encourage a student-centered environment. Classroom committees are introduced to the kids a few weeks into the new school year, once our daily routines have started to feel more familiar.

Initially, I assigned student committee spots myself. That failed for obvious reasons: the kids

POPSICLE STICKS: EQUALITY AND FAIRNESS

As a young student teacher, my supervisor caught me in a troubling practice that surprised me. As I taught, I called students at random. (At least, I believed I did!) I thought I was getting to everyone and varying my choices evenly. I was not. My supervisor tallied how often I called on each student, and I could see that it was uneven. Her advice: "Get popsicle sticks, and use them faithfully."

Now, in our room, popsicle sticks are incredibly powerful. Every student decorates their stick at the beginning of the year, and puts their name on one side. On the other side, they glue a magnet cut to the width of the stick, while the other end should remain blank and magnetless. The sticks

stay in a container and are cared for by the Stick Puller. Multiple classroom operations require the pulling of the sticks, including:

♥ Choosing the morning movement activities
♥ Picking seats for the week
♥ Selecting classroom jobs
♥ Answering questions during lessons
♥ Deciding partners
♥ Dividing the class into teams for whole group activities (with first two chosen as team captains)

I know, using popsicle sticks doesn't seem earth-shattering. I agree. However, those simple little pieces of wood guarantee an equal opportunity for everyone in the classroom. The randomness of pulling sticks makes sure that all students see that they are being chosen fairly.

didn't have any choice in the matter. I didn't know the students or their skill sets well enough for the committees to be successful. I tried letting the students nominate each other—failure number two. The kids nominated their friends because that's what kids do. However, committee members have to be able to work with each other for much longer than some student friendships last.

The selection process that finally worked—and is still in place currently—is the tried and true pulling of popsicle sticks. It's a fair and equal opportunity for each student to make a decision for themselves. It's empowering to identify an area of personal strength and choose a committee that needs that specific skill set.

I have always seen committees as an entirely different concept to classroom jobs. Jobs change each week. Committees are designed for members to develop a deeper skill level while working with their team on a consistent basis. They become the experts or specialists for the classroom. The class depends on committee members for leadership, help, or guidance when a need arises.

One year, during the winter holiday season, a door decorating competition developed. It started with one classroom door being decorated, and then it spread to others. It quickly became a heated competition. Whose door would be most festive? The creative battle was on! I gathered the Holiday Planner Committee together, and we cruised the halls to check out our competitors' doors. The Holiday Planners searched the internet for the coolest door idea they could find, then presented their idea to the class. Everyone took part in the creation of our door masterpiece under the direction of the Holiday Planner committee members. The specialists coordinated the entire operation from

Fifth graders are sticklers for fairness, as are students of many ages. Anything that seems unjust will be spotted quickly. The popsicle sticks ensure that no students feel targeted or overlooked. I promise. I believe wholeheartedly in their use because I have never, ever heard any student or their parents say that I show preferential treatment to one student over another. Really, never. Not once.

beginning to end. It was epic! Our finished holiday door was a sight to behold. Needless to say, ours was the best. Not only was it unbelievably amazing, it was also the only decorated holiday door done entirely by the kids. All I did was supervise the chaos and buy a few necessary materials. The students designed, created, and collaboratively built our classroom door (and part of the walls surrounding it) into a winter wonderland snowglobe.

The Holiday Decorator Committee oversees the decoration of the classroom door.

Here's the most important thing I've learned from my experience with classroom committees: they are only as meaningful and useful as they are made to be. They must be purposefully used with fidelity at every opportunity for the students to feel their contributions are valued. Could I do everything that the committees do on my own? Sure, I could. But, would that be creating choice and amplifying autonomy for my students? No, it wouldn't.

In order to be certain that committees are successful, vital, useful additions to the classroom environment, I set clear guidelines, and we stick to them. I resist the urge to just jump in and take care of a situation—no matter how big or how small— and let the student committees perform the tasks that are in their realm.

We have a large desktop calendar in the front of the room that our Secretary manages. I meet with the committees that have date-specific tasks, and we add them to the class calendar. Each morning, our Secretary reads off any extra items of information for the day. Some committees meet more regularly and have more duties than others. Party Planners only meet four or five times per year as classroom events arise on the calendar. Holiday Decorator meetings are written down at the beginning of every month as the room transitions from season to season or holiday to holiday. They are also active almost daily to maintain any decorative problems that require attention. Equipment Managers are on call consistently as needs arise within their scope of responsibilities. They add their dates for extra assistance to the class calendar when the younger students need extra P.E. help for bowling or roller skating. The members of the Tech Department meet with me frequently as new websites are introduced to the class. The Technicians are the first students who have contact with different sites and platforms. They spend time working together to understand and troubleshoot any issues before the whole class joins. Classroom jobs serve a daily need. Classroom committees focus on working together as a team throughout a designated period of nine weeks or even a whole semester.

CLASSROOM COMMITTEES

PARTY PLANNERS

Personality type: Organizers

Area of responsibility: Planning and supervising events for classroom parties

Duties:

- ♥ Pulling sticks to choose for which holiday they bring treats
- ♥ Making the poster for party names
- ♥ Passing out the notes for parties and coordinating the treats/drinks
- ♥ Facilitating the voting decision for movie selections
- ♥ Prepping for classroom parties
- ♥ Assisting during the events

HOLIDAY DECORATORS

Personality type: Creative, artistic students

Area of responsibility: Seasonal decoration of our classroom door three times per year

Duties:

- ♥ Bringing the seasonal decorations out of storage
- ♥ Facilitating the decoration of the room for the month/season
- ♥ Maintaining the decorations while they are up in the room
- ♥ Managing the creation of any seasonal door decorating contests
- ♥ Overseeing the condition of the decorations as they are put away

EQUIPMENT MANAGERS

Personality type: Interested in athletics

Area of responsibility: Balls and supplies for recess, games, and physical education equipment

Duties:

- ♥ Inflating and maintaining recess balls
- ♥ Gathering any supplies or belongings left on the playground
- ♥ Door holding for any extra recess time
- ♥ Assisting the P.E. teacher at the end of class time

TECH DEPARTMENT

Personality type: Technical problem-solvers

Area of responsibility: Troubleshooting and maintaining classroom technology. These are the skilled computer helpers.

Duties:

- ♥ Being first to learn how to log into different platforms so they can assist others when necessary
- ♥ Helping others get logged into websites we use
- ♥ Troubleshooting minor issues others may have
- ♥ Assisting students who have questions about how to use the computers
- ♥ Checking the computer cart and counting devices at the end of the day
- ♥ Trying out sites that the teacher may be interested in using
- ♥ Aiding any substitute teachers who aren't comfortable with the technology

JOBS AND COMMITTEES
HELP STUDENTS THRIVE

I never imagined that creating ways for my students to be involved in the daily operations of our classroom would have produced the effects that I've seen. I didn't understand how much my students wanted to feel like they were contributing members of the classroom.

The positive effects of classroom jobs are clearly evident in the notes that substitute teachers leave at the end of their day with my students. Here are some examples:

Great Class Friday.

The hardest working + best behaved class

Elementary + High School combined.

Thanks for having me

All went well! Your students were very helpful. I was impressed with their listening skills. That isn't true of all 6th graders in the area. I enjoyed the day.

When substitute teachers leave positive notes like these, something is going right.

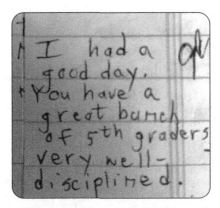

Another sub leaves a positive note.

I have numerous conversations with parents about their students' reactions to classroom jobs. Kids go home and talk about the jobs they like most, which jobs they want to have, and how important the job is. My favorite parent comment about jobs came via phone call.

"Could you please help him out?" the exasperated parent asked me. Well, of course, I answered, "But what do you need me to do?" The parent asked me to explain to the child that he needed to stay home if he was ill—even if he was excited about being Line Leader for the week. Students get very emotionally attached to their jobs! I made a deal with the child to extend his Line Leader position into the next week due to illness. He agreed with that solution, and his parents were thrilled to finish fighting him about attending school while he was sick.

Experiences like this continue to remind me how important jobs are to the students. Classroom jobs and committees help students feel a sense of belonging. They feel that they're making a genuine difference in the way our day runs. Offering opportunities for students to choose jobs gives the kids a purposeful task that benefits our entire classroom environment.

ISABELLE: Were there any positive or negative experiences you had with teachers growing up that led you to teach the way you do now?

GINA: My educational experiences have been overwhelmingly positive. I was an above-average student. School is what I did well. Most things came fairly easy to me. That was my strength, that was what I excelled at. I never had a problem with any of my teachers. I never gave any thought to what anybody around me went through. It didn't touch me, and of course, you're pretty self-centered when you're a kid, so I never ever noticed if others were struggling. While I was taking my education classes, the people that I considered to be closest and dearest to me shared some of the experiences they had in school.

GINA: I think a lot of those narratives have shaped the way that I see things, even now. I remember stories that people told me about, "I dropped out of high school and nobody ever said anything to me; I just turned in my books one day and everybody just let me go." I've got friends that have said, "Nobody ever really acted like I had any kind of an input into anything, and if teachers would have just given me a chance to try other things it might have made a difference to me." And those snapshots of experiences that happened in school make a huge difference to adults who still remember the feelings. They become thoughts that shape the way they see their own children's education. I think that's the real loss. Just think about it for a minute. If there could've been something that might have altered somebody's perception of their abilities when they were in school and they didn't get that opportunity. The way they perceived themself was changed and then it affected the way their future unrolled. Then someday, it affects the way their kids' educational perceptions are developed. It's a horrible legacy to perpetuate.

CHAPTER FOUR

Classroom Coupons

C lassroom coupons have been a staple of my class for years. They came into existence due to an incredibly competitive group of kids one year. There was a core group of boys who had competed in a variety of sports with and against each other for years. The girls were equally active. Many of them were softball and soccer players, and one was a competitive swimmer. I knew they loved sports and games because I watched them during recess. I wanted to see that same gusto and fire in the classroom.

I had tried incorporating different learning games, but the reactions were lackluster. I just couldn't seem to spark the engagement that I had seen on the playground. One day, at the end of a spelling activity, the boy who won seemed unimpressed with his outcome. Hoping that I could find a way to pump up his accomplishment, I suggested a coupon-type reward for his hard work and effort. His eyes lit up! The invention of coupons made the entire class work harder to learn facts and concepts that I would embed in a variety of classroom games. Those students quickly became eager, engaged, and in love with any type of educational classroom game or competition that I could invent. The coupons brought out the gusto and the fire that I had hoped for.

HOW AND WHY OF COUPONS

The coupons serve both sides of the motivational coin. The classroom games and learning activities are fun and challenging, so the kids are intrinsically engaged, and winning a coupon meets the extrinsic motivation at the end of the game. I believe that students benefit when both intrinsic and extrinsic motivations come together. Practicing and reviewing concepts using a variety of games motivates students just as much as winning coupons at the end of the activity.

I believe that students benefit when both intrinsic and extrinsic motivations come together.

To this day, most of the coupons in our room are given as a result of winning a game-type learning activity. The top three individuals with the highest scores at the end of online games get coupons, and if there are teams, I award them to all members of the winning group. In activities that need more than three or more teams, then the top two teams all get coupons. Students with winning streaks of a certain amount of correct answers can also get them.

Coupons can also be used in unexpected situations when genuinely helpful kids perform a task without being asked. Kids who are mentioned by other teachers for kind acts earn coupons. Sometimes students are singled out by other staff members for being kind, using great manners, or showing exemplary behavior. I make a note of those compliments, so students get coupons too.

The beauty of coupons is their ability to be applied in any way you wish. Coupons can be earned for various reasons, besides winning learning games. Students who are especially helpful if we have a substitute teacher in our room receive coupons. As long as the standards for receiving coupons remain attainable but not too easy, coupons are special rewards worth striving for.

They're also incredibly simple. I print copies as we need them, cut them apart, and store them in a plastic container near my chair. The students keep track of their coupons in an envelope kept in their milk crates. I collect names of students on slips of paper and stuff them in the coupon container. Once per week, on a designated day (Thursday for us), I spread the coupons out and call up a few kids at a time to select the one they want.

By now, you must be wondering, "what in the world do these coupons do for kids that make them so desirable?" The coupons give students the choice to do all sorts of things that appeal specifically to them. There are coupons for classroom jobs, alternative seating choices, classwork help, and other situations that students have suggested.

It's my low-tech way of gamifying the classroom. Retail rewards programs motivate customers to purchase based on the rewards they can earn; coupons work along the same motivational concept. They reward students for doing something I want them to do by earning privileges in class that are important to them. One of the best parts of this coupon system? I don't have to spend a small fortune buying trinkets and prizes to incentivize them to learn. My students want these classroom privileges more than any material objects. Whether you teach primary grades or older students, if you can identify what students want and provide a learning-based pathway to get it, you can find a motivational tool that works.

If you can identify what students want and provide a learning-based pathway to get it, you can find a motivational tool that works.

THE CLASSROOM COUPON LIST

CLASSROOM JOB COUPONS

♥ Pick your classroom job first: Choose the job you want the most before someone else can.

♥ Take over another person's job for the week: Take someone's job if they picked the one you wanted, then they pick again.

♥ Cannot have my classroom job taken: Protect a favorite classroom job from being stolen through someone else's coupon.

♥ Job guarantee: Confirm your choice of job for the week. The first student to turn in a job guarantee coupon on Friday goes first on Monday. This coupon is unique to students who miss school for appointments on Monday mornings and don't get to pick the job they want. By turning the coupon in on Friday, they get the job they want on Monday morning even if they aren't at school.

SEATING COUPONS

♥ Reserve your seat: Confirm where you'll sit for the week. This coupon must be turned in before our weekly seat selection. Reserve seat coupons are used before "Pick your spot first" coupons.

♥ Pick your spot first: This coupon allows the holder to pick a spot before sticks are pulled.

♥ Change seats: Switch seats with anyone.

❧ Reverse the change seat coupon: Regain the spot you wanted, reversing the change seat coupon. (The kids have always been good-natured about reversal coupons. They understand that's just how it works sometimes.)

CHOOSE FIRST COUPONS

❧ First to use a coupon: Use a coupon first the next day. This coupon needs to be turned in the afternoon prior. It was created to help everyone have a fair chance to use their coupons without being affected by differing arrival times (i.e., kids who ride the bus).

❧ Be the first for everything all day: Be first to line up, the front of the line, and first for anything else all day long.

❧ Question priority: Your questions get immediate attention and are answered first all day.

❧ Go Noodle picker: Choose all three of the morning movement videos.

STUDENT PRIVILEGE COUPONS

❧ New school supply item: Choose something new from the school supply basket, like extra crayons or markers. This coupon benefits students who need something from the basket, maybe because their family couldn't buy it, as well as kids who just want to choose new school supplies.

❧ Computer pass: Choose your favorite school-appropriate sites and games for one day after your classwork is done.

- Inside recess: Stay inside and play with one friend. On nasty weather days, staying in the classroom can be nice.
- Line jumper: Pick your spot in line and cut in line to any spot all day.
- Lunch date with the teacher: Check the lunch menu with the teacher, pick a friend, and eat together in the cafeteria at a separate table.
- Bring a drink: Bring any drink to enjoy during independent reading time except for soda pop. They can already have water.
- Bring a snack: Bring an individual snack to eat during independent reading time. Students can't share with others or pass snacks around.

STUDENT APPAREL COUPONS

- Wear a hat: Wear any hat in our class all day, as long as it doesn't cause distractions to yourself or others.
- Wear slippers: Wear your favorite slippers in class all day, as long as it doesn't cause distractions to yourself or others.
- Wear sunglasses: Wear sunglasses in the classroom, as long as it doesn't cause distractions to yourself or others.
- Assignment Coupons
- "Only do half the assignment" pass: Eliminates half the work on a daily practice work assignment. This coupon is only used at the teacher's discretion based on student understanding of the content.

❤ Skip spelling words: Skip one or two spelling words on a spelling test.

❤ Add two points to any assignment: Add points in the grade book to a specific assignment.

❤ Work with a friend on an assignment: Get help from another student on a chosen assignment. This coupon is also up to the teacher's discretion based on the assignment and the coupon holders.

CLASSROOM GAME COUPONS

❤ Scorekeeper for an activity: Serve as scorekeeper and host of a chosen in-class game (usually spelling games).

❤ Boost team score: Add three points to any team score at the end of an in-class game.

Coupons add an extra layer of motivation.

GUIDELINES FOR COUPONS

There are a few small guidelines that I've put in place over time. I only issue coupons once per week. Otherwise, it feels like a never-ending chore. All coupons have to have my initials, the student's name, and the date to be valid. It keeps coupons from being misappropriated by kids.

I don't hold onto coupons from one day to the next unless it's designed to be used that way. The kids have to turn them in to me in the morning before our day begins. Students may use as many coupons per day as they wish to use.

Coupon usage can be denied in certain cases. If the students are practicing a skill set that they may be having problems with, then they can't use the "only do half of the assignment" coupon or the "work with a partner" coupons.

Coupons that aren't used properly can be declared null and void. For example, once when I was absent for a few days, the kids used their computer pass coupons that allow for "school-appropriate games." However, the games many of them were playing were, in fact, not school appropriate. The substitute teacher mentioned some of those games in the note she left for me. Based on the improper usage of the coupons, that particular one was declared useless for an undetermined amount of time.

The kids are in charge of their own coupons. If they get damaged or lost, there's no replacement process.

At the end of the year, if the students have coupons that they haven't used, they can be turned in for extra recess time.

COUPONS MOTIVATE AND ENGAGE STUDENTS

Coupons continue to be sought after each year, primarily because they are specifically geared toward the kids' unique tastes. Student input in the creation of new coupons keeps them fresh and interesting. Every year, I encourage students to submit ideas to add to the list of choices. Their voices are evident in each coupon. What they generate can get pretty far out of the realm of possibility at times. Obviously, certain ideas are worth giving a run at, but teacher common sense prevails. "No distractions to the learning environment" is my only guideline for offering a new coupon option for consideration.

Coupons are an easy way to encourage students' choices in making autonomous decisions. They propose new coupon ideas, and they independently decide on the coupons they want most when they have earned them. Then they pick when it's most advantageous to use them. Even simple decisions are important when you're a kid. Big decisions are easier when students have practice making a lot of smaller decisions. Plus, fifth graders are incredibly competitive. Rewarding highest scores, correct answer streaks, and winning teams ensures focused and concentrated effort during practice game activities in class.

Ask yourself: What do I want to incentivize my students to do? What privileges or benefits would really motivate them? How can I create a system to motivate students to do classroom activities with those incentives? Your system doesn't have to be complex, either. My coupon system has evolved over the years; it wasn't this intricate in the beginning. Start small. Do what works for you. Involve your students in the process. In the end, you may end up creating something that makes your students look forward to class activities in a new way.

ISABELLE: I know a lot of your book is about your teaching style and how other teachers can do it, but have you always taught like this? Tell me about the process that led up to where you are now.

GINA: This is going to sound really odd, but it always felt like the things I was trying made sense. I think it's important for people to understand that it took years to figure out some of this stuff. It just kind of became a constant search for how to make students as comfortable as possible in situations so they can learn best, and how to give them some choices and some autonomy. The ideas that I tried either failed miserably or worked well, and I thought, "This feels so much more natural for me, so much more natural for the kids."

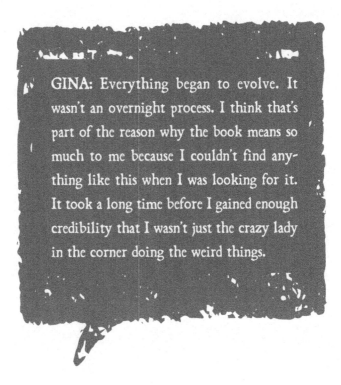

GINA: Everything began to evolve. It wasn't an overnight process. I think that's part of the reason why the book means so much to me because I couldn't find anything like this when I was looking for it. It took a long time before I gained enough credibility that I wasn't just the crazy lady in the corner doing the weird things.

CREATING
A CLASSROOM

I used to drive myself crazy trying to make my room look perfect. I was obsessed. Other teachers posted pictures of their rooms on social media. I believed that mine had to look similar to theirs, or I was doing something horribly wrong.

Eventually, I realized I had wasted a ton of time. I missed the fact that the kids needed to be part of the creation of our space in order to have ownership of it. Now, the students and I build our classroom from scratch. My kids are empowered stakeholders in decision-making.

Hold this idea in the back of your mind as you read:

How can I use these ideas to create my own classroom with my students?

CHAPTER FIVE

Our Classroom, Our Home

Our classroom is our home. It's where my students and I live and learn five days a week.

I developed this "classroom as a home" concept subconsciously. I didn't realize the reasons I created it that way until another teacher asked me to explain. I told her that I was filling a need for myself and for my kids. I didn't realize how profound that was until I heard it come out of my mouth.

Generations ago, school was school. Home was home. However, over time, society and family dynamics have changed. For many students, home doesn't look the same now as it did when I was growing up.

Here's an example: My parents started dating in high school. They married shortly after my mom graduated, and they've stayed married since March 1965. We lived at the same address the entire time I was in school. My dad worked one full-time job on our family farm, where his hours varied a bit seasonally, but his schedule was reliable. My mom never worked outside the home. With few exceptions, we ate our evening meal together every night of the year at 6 p.m. In the evening, all of the kids did their homework. If any of us needed assistance, both of my parents were there to help. We all had bedtimes, and we had to stick to them with no distractions allowed. Everyone woke up in the morning, and the day began again.

I had advantages as a student: reliability, consistency, parental involvement. These are almost incomparable to the experiences of many of my students.

Some kids don't have much of a home life when school lets out. So our classroom took on many of those homey aspects to help fill a void for my students. I want us to feel relaxed and safe when we're in the classroom. It needs to be a place that feels like us.

GET YOUR PRIORITIES STRAIGHT TO BUILD COMMUNITY

That feeling of home doesn't stop with the look and design of the room. I am a firm believer in building a strong sense of community in the classroom. The social and emotional growth of my students is a priority. Establishing a genuine, caring atmosphere where all learners feel safe, comfortable, and valued is a fifth-grade classroom necessity.

It all starts at the beginning. Welcome students. Set them at ease. It's vital for establishing positive classroom expectations.

Students need to feel a sense of belonging in order to become healthy, successful individuals who can build relationships. This is true for all kids. We can assume that students will just find their own way, but that will not guarantee a sense of belonging. Students need to feel purposefully connected to a classroom. The year begins with a clean slate for everyone. EVERYONE. That means I won't read students' cumulative folders, you know—those files that get passed along from grade to grade with reports on each student.

YOU CAN'T BUILD COMMUNITY WITH WHAT IF'S

Over a summer, a transfer student was added to my roster. He was rumored to be a "problem child." I broke my rule and read his cumulative file.

It was a mistake. It was bad. Really bad.

I fretted a bit. Worried a bit more. What would I do if this kid was as awful as the records indicated? I imagined all of the same volatile situations that the file contained. By the time the year was ready to actually start, I was far down the what-if rabbit hole.

I met him that first morning, and we began our day. I felt nervous and unnaturally paranoid as I waited for something to happen. Then, nothing did. It never came. He was a normal-ish, regular-like fifth-grade boy.

I had freaked myself out. I had made the mistake of reading his file and letting its contents and my speculation run rampant in my mind. I almost made the even bigger mistake of letting someone else tell me through his file how our relationship would be.

Sometimes, we assume how a student will behave based on what we've seen with our own two eyes. That's still a big assumption. It doesn't mean that he behaves that way when he graces the doorstep of your classroom. So, I don't read the records with the anecdotal comments written about incoming students. I want to meet my students with a clean slate. I prefer not to have any preconceived notions about them.

I want to meet my students with a clean slate. I prefer not to have any preconceived notions about them.

Case in point: Over a four-year period, every time I had recess duty, there was this *one kid*. He always had my attention. He consistently broke rules, and that didn't bother him. He liberally shared his incredibly loud opinions every time he got written up for a rule infraction during recess. I have no idea how many times I wrote that kid up and followed him to his classroom to speak with his teacher. I dreaded having him as a fifth grader in my room.

I was completely, utterly wrong again. Apparently, the environment and management style of my classroom was a perfect fit for him. He was bright and intuitive. His background knowledge on a variety of topics enriched most classroom discussions. His sense of humor was a bit more developed than most kids. We discovered that we shared some unusual favorite television shows. He was eager to learn, especially from his mistakes. His work ethic earned him the growth mindset award from his fifth-grade peers. He was a fabulous kid, and we had a great year! If I had let my own preconceptions get in the way of actually getting to know him, it could have ruined the whole experience for both of us.

DESTROYING FEARS PHYSICALLY AND METAPHORICALLY

Based on those experiences, we start the year differently now. On the first day of fifth grade, we all, myself included, write down our worries. I'm also nervous and anxious at the beginning of the year. It's a communal, humanizing experience that we all have together. We write about fears we may have. We write about what didn't go well the previous year. In pairs, students go to the trash can, tear up their worries, and shred the issues from last year. Destroying the pieces of paper and throwing them away symbolically frees us up, so we can start fresh. The year is going to be different because we have faced our past issues and vowed not to let them rule us again. We don't share those fears with anyone. We have ripped them up, and they no longer have any power over us. We have dealt with and discarded them. It acknowledges the past and sets a new intention for future growth. No one feels trapped into repeating the same mistakes from last year. We are cleaning the slate and starting new.

COLLABORATIVE CLASSROOM DECORATION

Before the kids arrive at the beginning of the school year, I tidy the room. I unstack the chairs and tables. I spruce up the bookshelves. With respect to classroom decorating, I do two things before school starts. I cover our job board with want ads from our local newspaper, and I hang a welcome sign on the door. That is all I do—at least right away.

I used to download and save cute ideas for classroom decor. My desktop folders were chock full of screenshotted pictures. I bought stuff. Ordered items. Saw more creative examples from others. Screenshotted them, too. Made more desktop folders. Then I bought more stuff.

I could have burned through a whole laminator myself. I used to give up many of my last few days of summer to the noble teacher mantra of "working on the room," so it was picture-perfect. Pinterest perfect.

I want my classroom to be a family, not a themed event based on a popular movie or a social media craze.

It was grueling, not to mention expensive. I honestly thought that was what I was supposed to do. It seemed to be what others were doing, so I adopted the same behaviors.

I guess I'm not entirely sure what the benefits of the magical "picture-perfect" classroom were supposed to be. Why had I driven myself moderately bonkers over all of the decorating? What did the cutsie posters and wall hangings do? Was the wow factor of a bulletin board something that meant I was a good teacher? Did anyone really care what my classroom theme or colors were? Would others think badly of me if everything wasn't ideal?

Teachers will use many themes when they are setting up their classrooms. I've never thought that went deep enough. I want my classroom to be a family, not a themed event based on a popular movie or a social media craze.

So one year, I stopped. All of it. Instead, I tried an experiment. I waited for my students to arrive, and we decorated our classroom. Together.

As it turned out, my experimentation had actual benefits. Working and decorating together with my students let me get to know them. It let my kids burn off much of their nervous anxiety about beginning a new year. I gleaned insights into their strengths and uniqueness. I met these hidden artistic creators, creative thinkers, and imaginative designers. I saw the beginnings of teamwork. I took notice of friendships. I watched for leadership abilities and observed risk-takers. It was so much more fun than I imagined it would be.

Perhaps the greatest benefit of collaborative classroom decoration was the sense of belonging and ownership the kids exhibited. The classroom they styled and arranged did something very valuable. It celebrated and honored their individual creativity. Their ideas were valued. The students were authentic contributors to our space. Therefore, they were ardently devoted to the care and upkeep of our classroom.

All kids need to realize they have something of value to share with others. Everyone wants to feel like they are valued by their peers. Giving the students opportunities to find or develop skills that are inherent to them helps tremendously. Observing daily interactions, taking note of their talents and abilities, and complimenting their areas of strength empowers them. Computer aptitude, leadership qualities, and organizational tendencies are examples of valuable skills that can be identified by focusing on students' behaviors, actions, and responses. Kids are surprised and flattered when I mention how their specific talents will be helpful to me, their peers, and our classroom. Their unique personalities and perspectives are welcome in our new fifth-grade home.

This is the making of a classroom community, whether it's done by slaying fears, giving students a clean slate, choosing priorities carefully, or co-creating the physical classroom space.

Letting students decorate the room? Yep, it was the right decision. Build your classroom with your students, not for them. Set it up together so it belongs to all of you.

At the end of the year, this is what Noah wrote for the next class of fifth graders to know: "Treat the classroom like it's home." Because it is!

Riley's reflections on the ideal classroom:

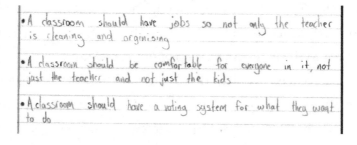

- A classroom should have jobs so not only the teacher is cleaning and organising

- A classroom should be comfortable for everyone in it, not just the teacher and not just the kids

- A classroom should have a voting system for what they want to do

ISABELLE: Obviously, your teaching style is very unique, which I'm sure has brought you some criticisms from fellow teachers, parents, administrators, etc. How have you been able to deal with any criticisms you've received over the years?

GINA: It was hard in the early days because I was new and I was doing odd things. In a school, if you're doing things differently, people are going to take notice of that. There are times where people are very cautious and very unsure about the way I was changing things. There's always going to be some people that are uncertain. However, the relationships and the things that can't be quantified are the things that mean the most. At the end of the day, it's truly that connective piece that makes all the difference in the world. As long as that piece existed, and inherently grew, there weren't any issues with parents or anyone else. Then it became kind of cool that I was over here dimming lights, skyping with Africa, and trying all those other things.

CHAPTER SIX

Alternative Seating

One of my earliest fifth-grade physical classrooms as a teacher was full of desks. They were awkward, boxcar-shaped, rectangular things that consumed all of the space in the room. I hoped to arrange them to make the room feel less institutional and restrictive. The sheer size and number of the boxcars made moving around difficult. Towards the back, looming in a corner, was an even larger wooden structure that was supposed to be the teacher's desk.

SQUATTERS AND TIPPERS. OH MY!

The space was a traditional classroom in every sense of the concept. I moved my belongings in and began to valiantly shove the unwieldy furnishings into some sort of an arrangement. I tried every combination of positions and groupings I could think of. The desks still overwhelmed the classroom. I tried not to let the cramped surroundings quash my enthusiasm as I set up my desk and decorated the space.

Once the year began, and my students were settled, everything was supposed to progress in a normal, school-like fashion. But, I began to notice weird things.

For one, I had a squatter.

He was a bright kid with eager eyes and consistently disheveled blond hair. No matter how many times I requested, encouraged, and finally angrily ordered him to, he could not—would not!—sit in his blue school-issued chair. He would begrudgingly attempt to comply, but minutes later, he would squat like a frog on the blue plastic lilypad. People behind him couldn't see, and his incessant moving was disrupting his neighbors.

I soon developed some tippers. When they saw my ineffective efforts to stop the squatter from squatting, they constantly leaned back on their chairs. I was certain that eventually, they would tip too far and fall backward. The concussions they would suffer would be completely my fault.

Soon, most of my time was spent trying to curb the seating issues. Something needed to change because they were quickly developing into larger behavioral problems.

I was obsessed. I read articles and hunted for any classroom management tips or tricks that could possibly help get things back under control.

That's how alternative seating became an integral part of my classroom environment—and, eventually, something else that gave my students autonomy and voice in our classroom.

No one learns best in situations where they are uncomfortable. That applies to everyone, everywhere. At building-wide professional development sessions, teachers arrive noisily, bringing their own comfy chairs from their rooms with them. It's the same concept for students. Kids have to feel safe and comfortable before any true learning can happen.

FIRST SEATING ATTEMPTS

My first flexible seating options were simple. I grabbed a few old couch cushions from my basement and hauled them to school, swapping them out for some of the clunky boxcars. I tripped across a couple of inflatable exercise discs at a garage sale, aired them up, and introduced them to my tippers. The squatter received an ottoman—to squat on to his heart's content—along with a spot in the back row to prevent blocking others.

This first round of alternative seating experiments taught me a few things.

For one, you don't have to order pricey wobble chairs or wiggle stools from a catalog to offer seating alternatives. Anything can work. If you're handy, build something (but be sure it's sturdy!). If you know what you're trying to accomplish, pick something students can sit on that might do the trick. No matter the grade level or content area, this simple strategy—knowing what you want to accomplish and picking something to address it—can help customize the classroom for your unique students.

Another lesson learned: the right seating can alter relationships and classroom dynamics. With the addition of the new seats, power struggles over seating behaviors disappeared. If they were at ease, learning unfamiliar concepts and practicing new skills seemed to be less of a struggle for my students.

The right seating can alter relationships and classroom dynamics.

Altering the students' seating choices was a success for the kids and for me. Based on the positive results, my classroom environment looks less traditional year after year.

TRANSITIONING THE TEACHER DESK

I discovered that my students felt like they were "in trouble" when they needed to come to the teacher's desk. It was a daunting, unwelcoming structure. So, I removed the stigma for them and found something that seemed more natural.

The enormous teacher's desk was hauled out, and I replaced it with my favorite items from my late grandfather's den: the ugliest olive green swivel rocker in the entire world, accompanied by an ancient, fake leather ottoman on wheels.

I paired them with an elderly end table from a consignment shop that holds a small supply of frequently used items. My laptop, notepad, and box of markers fit on top of the ottoman nicely.

I have no regrets about getting rid of my unwieldy teacher desk. Here's why:

▶ I realized that most of the stuff in or on the recently defunct teacher desk wasn't vital. In fact, a lot of it was unnecessary junk.

▶ Transitioning from the monster desk to the swivel rocker felt liberating.

▶ I didn't feel as separated from the students as I had while sitting behind the wooden bastion.

When I got rid of my teacher desk, it was liberating.

Untethering myself from my teacher's desk made me more accessible to my students and strengthened my connections to them. Students started approaching the ugly chair and sitting down on the floor beside the ottoman when they had questions or confusion. It didn't seem to be quite as intimidating as facing the dreaded teacher desk. I worked with many more kids than I had before. If there was a group of students with similar questions, they all sat down in a semi-circle around the front of the ugly chair while I grabbed a marker board and did some reteaching. Changing my perspective and proximity was a decision that I have never regretted.

TRANSITIONING THE CLASSROOM

I've purchased most of my classroom seating items myself, generally at garage sales or thrift shops. I shop as inexpensively as possible because my students are kids. They break things. They spill. They have accidents. Expensive classroom items don't look pristine for long. I know that sounds obvious, but I've seen the results of teachers who get caught up in designing and forget this reality.

I taught next door to a woman who brought in personal items and objects to add to her room's decor. One afternoon, I heard a horrible ruckus. Scooting quickly next door, I was abruptly confronted with disaster. Three shelves had fallen off the wall, shards and pieces of broken objects littered the tile—all due to students being kids. The teacher was devastated, and the students felt horrible. She explained that most of the objects were gifts from friends and family. One of the items was hand-made by her late father. It was utterly irreplaceable.

There should never be any item brought into a classroom of kids that is irreplaceable. Murphy has a law for a reason. I have never kept track of the amount of items that headed to the great dumpster in the sky from my classroom. The loss is not worth remembering. There are kids in my room, and I expect that things will happen. You should too.

What I have learned about selecting items:

> ▸ **Milk crates are the hidden secret to flexible seating.** Gather enough milk crates, so every student in the classroom has one, and have a few hidden away for kids that move in later. The students keep all of their

classroom supplies in milk crates, which sit on the floor next to their chosen spot. Using milk crates does require the usage of pencil boxes or pencil cases to hold crayons, markers, or other writing utensils, but they hold everything else. Students can easily move their milk crates around during class based on different activities. At the end of the day, all the crates get stacked in the front of the room. I've found them to be the perfect storage companion to alternative seats. As an added benefit, they're easy to clean out or straighten up.

▶ **Always think about things that may go awry before choosing items to bring into the classroom.** I found a long, low-backed homely couch in my favorite consignment shop. It was perfectly sized for kids. The proprietor knew I was planning on using it in the classroom, so she discounted the price to twenty-five dollars. I was overjoyed! When we got the couch to the building, I learned that the school's rules had changed. Any different or new furniture additions to classrooms had to have documentation that proved the furniture had been treated with a specialized fire retardant. I whined to no avail, tied the couch back up, and headed home to the garage. The couch is living in my garage to this day. Some extra pondering or discussion could have helped me avoid all of this.

► **Cheap is great, sturdy is better.** It was at a different thrift shop that I found these three green cloth-covered cubes. Their lids came off and there was storage inside. The tops were padded for seating. They were cheap. Like, really cheap. Excited by my lucky find, I hauled them into the classroom. All three of them were in the dumpster two months later because the sides weren't sturdy enough.

► **Garage sales are classroom gold mines.** Look for family yard sales with kid's items. By the time a family decides to sell chairs that their children have outgrown, those chairs have passed all the kid tests. You know they are tough and sturdy enough to survive! Long, long ago, I came across two hard plastic, video game-style floor chairs at a garage sale. I paid next to nothing for both of them. Those two chairs have outlasted many other classroom items by years. They are still in good shape and in active use as of today.

► **Comfort knows no color scheme.** Hunting for items to include in your alternative seating choices must be done with the kids' needs in mind. Students don't care whether or not the seat follows a color scheme or looks good with the other pieces in the room. Their only concerns are whether it's comfortable and they can work well while sitting in it.

ALTERNATIVE SEATING THAT HAS WORKED BEST IN MY CLASSROOM:

- ♥ Low tables: Tables with the extension piece of the legs removed, letting kids sit on the floor
- ♥ Round, flat, exercise discs: Can be used in a chair or on the floor
- ♥ Hokki stools: Allow lots of movement due to the rounded bottom
- ♥ Hard plastic floor rockers: Can be moved anywhere around the room and are easy to clean
- ♥ Small tents: A huge kid favorite, great for introverted kids
- ♥ Hanging canopies: Loved by introverted kids, allow some seclusion from the large, expansive classroom
- ♥ Small trampolines: Let kids gently bounce while working
- ♥ Standing desks: Appeal to certain kids; either they love them or hate them
- ♥ Accent chairs: Fireproofed (of course; remember my garage couch), straight-backed ones, regular rockers, and swivel rockers

ALTERNATIVE SEATING THAT DID NOT WORK IN MY CLASSROOM:

- ♥ Bean bags: Flatten out quickly. Once the beans are flattened, the seat is unusable, and replacing them is a huge mess. I tried once and wound up with beans everywhere, so I had to borrow a vacuum from the custodians.
- ♥ Backrest seats: The ones with the beans go flat way too soon.
- ♥ Floor seats with hinged backs: The hinges break easily from all of the adjusting and leaning that kids do. Tippers will still be tippers.
- ♥ Lap desks: Just never became a useful choice that kids were drawn to.

I do have some pricey alternative seating pieces. They have been the results of graciously funded projects from different crowdsourcing sites for teachers. The standing desk, some of the taller wobble seats, the trampolines, and the tent are all examples of items that came from funded projects that I proposed. If you're short on alternative seating ideas, check out some of the "teacher help" style crowdsourcing websites. They can be a viable option to add some new seating choices to the classroom.

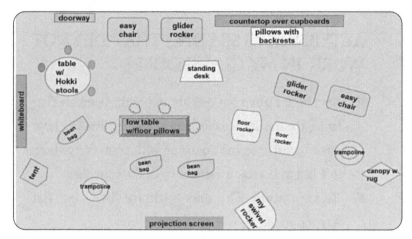

Ms. Ruffcorn's Classroom Layout

BE INTENTIONAL

Over time, my experiences with alternative seating have taught me to become very intentional in the selection of seating choices. Here's what I've learned about different choices we've made over the years:

> ► There are a few **accent chairs** that appeal to kids who prefer to curl up and feel comforted. These are the kind of chairs that can be found at consignment shops, auctions, or garage sales. They have high backs and sides, along with a generously cushioned seat. They are generally ugly and outdated based on popular styles of previous generations. If you grew up visiting your great aunts', or grandparents' homes, these are the kind of chairs you found in their front rooms. (Special note: check with your custodial staff to make sure you can bring in upholstered chairs based on fireproofing guidelines from your fire marshal.)

- The **low table** draws in the kids who frequently change positions. Often, kids who prefer to lay down as they read or work select the low table. On the floor, it makes no difference how many times they adjust or in what ways they choose to sit.

- The **tent and canopy** were both added to the classroom to fill a need for the introverted kids. Sometimes shy or introverted kids prefer to have a spot where they feel safer. During independent reading or working times, they can choose whether or not they want more privacy and some time away from the large group.

- Learners who enjoy rocking or swaying like the **wobble chairs**. Moving while they learn helps them to focus on the material being taught.

- Some kids prefer to stand, so they choose the **standing desk**.

As the needs of the students change, so should the alternative seating options. If you want to be intentional about the seating you offer your students, you might try a few things.

First, observe your students in a variety of settings. See where they sit, how they sit, if they sit, and what they do while there. These clues can help you pick the right seating option for those preferences. Students change. To some extent, preferences change too, but some are fairly universal among a grade or age group.

As the needs of the students change, so should the alternative seating options.

Second, ask your students. If we're trying to give them a voice and autonomy, this should be natural. We might not be able to accommodate all of their requests, but they can certainly guide decisions on new seating.

Third, talk to others. You might already know what your colleagues in your building think. Expand your perspective by talking to teachers in other schools and districts. Reach out through social media networks. Search for ideas and keep an eye on teacher's blogs and other places with real talk about what works and what doesn't.

SEATING GUIDELINES

We change seats on Monday mornings, using popsicle sticks to decide who gets to pick which seat.

I don't choose the spots for the students because that defeats the whole purpose of allowing them to explore and understand which type of seat or area is best for them as learners.

I've had the exact same seating guidelines since I implemented alternative seating. They're incredibly simple, and they give students freedom and a voice in their learning:

▶ Pick the spot that will work best for you as a learner. What kind of spot do you need to be comfortable, focused, and successful?

▶ If you have an issue with distracting others, you'll get one reminder to make better choices.

▶ If there is a need for a second reminder, I get to move you to a location of my choosing for the rest of the week.

▶ I reserve the right to veto a seating choice for students who have not picked spots that best suit them as learners.

FLEXIBLE SEATING = STUDENT CHOICE

Flexible seating is about student choice. They have to be the ones making the choices. The spots are meant to appeal to a wide variety of learners. Sometimes, they make good selections based on their needs, and it works well. Other times, kids make crappy choices because they want to sit by their buddy or be able to see up the hall. If they make a poor choice, by picking a seat where they can't work effectively, or they are distracting others, then they get one verbal reminder. If there's another issue, I choose a different place for them to sit for the week. Perhaps next week they will think twice and make a better selection.

Selecting their own spots allows the students to feel like they have some control over their environment. Alternative seating should never be used as a punishment or as a reward. It's important for students to experience the autonomy of choosing spots that work best for their needs. I trust them to make the right choices for themselves, and they trust me to let them try it. Flexibility in seating allows for easier accessibility for helping students and answering questions. Moving around the room and meeting the kids wherever they have chosen to work continues to build stronger connections with them.

Since flexible seating has become the norm in my classroom, I have continued to see how the students are positively affected. The second they have the ability to take ownership of their places in the classroom, the feeling of belonging begins to take root.

Feedback from my students has been overwhelmingly in favor of keeping flexible seating in fifth grade.

The best part of fifth grade was:

"The flexible seating because all of the seats are comfortable." Bella

"The chairs because not a lot of classrooms have them." Abe

"The cool chairs because I like to be comfy." Jayla

"You get to pick your own seats." Chloe

"There is comfortable seating and you get to sit where you want." Noah

ISABELLE: Results are definitely a big part of gaining that credibility. How would you describe the effect or impact of autonomy on a kid as they grow and develop?

GINA: I believe that giving kids choices, a voice in things, and giving them some autonomy and some decisions they can make for themselves transfers over to other classes and other experiences. I know the place still feels like home for a ton of kids because I still see high school and junior high kids regularly appear in my room. I think the environment makes a huge difference and knowing that everything isn't completely run, dictated, and managed by me not only helps me, but it helps them, too. I think a lot of classroom situations could really benefit from just some simple changes. It's not a lot. You don't have to buy anything, there's no program to learn, there's no steps you have to follow. It's just authentic, genuine, proven ideas that work in a classroom. I don't know if it makes any difference whether I've got fifth graders, third graders, or seniors; if you're offering them choices, ideas, and opportunities, so they feel like they've got a voice, I think it makes a huge difference no matter where you are.

CHAPTER SEVEN

Teacher-Tested, Kid-Approved Classroom Choices

We have all tried at one point or another to get a child to do something they don't want to do: practice an instrument, eat vegetables, go to bed on time, clean up a bedroom. The list is infinite. Best-case scenario: the endeavor is difficult. At the opposite end of the spectrum, the worst-case scenario is almost impossible. Hopefully, over time, with many tries, fails, and successes, we find a happy medium and discover a tried and approved method for accomplishing the tasks.

This chapter is full of my teacher-tested, kid-approved practices to give students some different options for autonomy and choice. They're the happy medium of my trial and error over the years. Hopefully, some of the ideas resonate with you and can easily be integrated into your own classroom.

FALLING OUT: INTENSIFIES PRODUCTIVITY

Alternative seating options help students feel comfortable. But they don't guarantee comfort for extended periods of time. Being able to disconnect from work when you personally need a break is a luxury both adults and children enjoy.

To be perfectly honest, I'm not sure when or where the term "falling out" developed. It's been a routine part of my classroom, and our vocabulary, for as long as I can remember. Falling out takes place anytime that kids are working, reading, or learning independently. If there's no need for everyone to focus on a concept being explained as a large group, the kids get to fall out. They can leave their regular seats, move around a bit, and settle into a different spot.

The only guideline to falling out: you can't distract others. Giving students the choice to leave their regular seats gives them a level of freedom that often only adults get. Some favorite spots to fall out include under the counter, between the bookshelves, or behind the easel. Once, I had students who put small pillows in the sink, sat on them, and worked there. Wherever kids can focus best without bothering anyone else is an independent decision for them to make.

I can't stay or sit in the same spot all day. Moving around and finding a new, comfortable place to work also makes me more focused and engaged. Independent reading is my favorite fall out time, personally. I stretch out on the floor with my book, comfortably settling in to read along with my kids.

> Being able to fall out has been mentioned frequently in response to the question, "What did you enjoy most about fifth grade?"
>
> "Being able to get up and move or stretch." Hannah
>
> "To be able to get out of your seat and move around." Mason
>
> "To sit around the class or move around the room." Mia
>
> "Picking your own spots to work." Chloe
>
> "We can sit where we want." Noah

MOVEMENT AND BREATHING: ACTIVATES THE BRAIN

Kids can be awkward. They are frequently impulsive. They easily become uncomfortable. Then, they begin to act out because they don't have the experience or stamina to understand how to handle those feelings.

So in our classroom, we incorporate lots of movement. Getting out of our seats and getting our minds and bodies moving helps us focus, be more productive, and eliminate disruptions.

Many years ago, our elementary staff attended an informational meeting hosted by a nurse from our local children's hospital. She introduced us to a website and, honestly, I was paying very little attention until she said one phrase: "deep breathing and yoga." I sat up straight and paid attention as she showed us a deep breathing video to try with kids.

My unconventional curiosity was piqued. I liked the idea of starting the day with some deep breathing and stretches to increase focus and attention. The next morning, I was an immediate fan. My kids and I started every day deep breathing and stretching. Over time, we started using GoNoodle (gonoodle. com)—a site with videos to get kids up and moving—to help with these exercises. Out of all the strategies, concepts, and acronyms that have come and gone over the years in my teaching career, GoNoodle is the one thing that has endured for me.

Fast-forward to the winter of 2016. GoNoodle was having a contest based on the "mannequin challenge." This was a popular social media craze where participants posed totally still while a video was recorded exploring the room. The winner of the contest would receive a personal visit from the GoNoodle celebrities and an all-school assembly. Since GoNoodle had become such a staple of our classroom, we knew we had to enter. Lots of ideas were bandied around until we had poses we all agreed on. We shot our video and tweeted it off to GoNoodle. Since all the entries were visible on Twitter, we watched other videos as they poured in from all over the United States. The kids were optimistic, and I tried to stress how slim the odds of us being chosen were. When the announcement was made, we were ecstatic. We won! The whooping of the fifth grade carried through the halls.

Since the whole elementary school was invited to the assembly, we had a big task on our hands. We needed to be the ambassadors of an elementary cultural overhaul. We had to get all of the other grades up and moving. And what was the core of our planning and decision-making? Student voice and autonomy, of course! We brainstormed and came up with a plan to reinfuse GoNoodle into the other classrooms. We divided our class into small groups. Each group was in charge of selecting GoNoodle activities that they would teach to the other classes. I held a small informational meeting and shared our plans with the elementary teachers. My kids were in charge of everything else. For weeks, the other elementary grades took turns and came to our room each morning to Go Noodle with their fifth-grade buddies. My kids loved sharing their favorite activities.

When the day of the assembly arrived, all of the kids celebrated together in the gym. My kids were excited to have won the contest, but they were also proud of having ignited a GoNoodle revolution in elementary.

My class was thrilled to win the GoNoodle contest.

We displayed our GoNoodle banner proudly.

The variety of GoNoodle activities positively impacted the classroom environments throughout the elementary school. Teachers reported that students were more focused and productive. Disruptive classroom behaviors decreased when GoNoodle was used regularly.

Implementing brain breaks can happen at any time during our day. Sometimes, I'll suggest a vote about whether or not we need to move. Other times, the kids will ask if they are in need of some movement. Never lose sight of the students and their needs. Using movement in our classroom is a necessity.

> Student feedback has consistently favored continuing the use of GoNoodle and other active brain breaks:
>
> "I like to get up and be able to move and stretch." Hannah
>
> "I need to get up and move every forty-five minutes to an hour." Sage
>
> "I like to have something to get us up and moving." Grace
>
> "The best part is the GoNoodles because it gets us super active in the morning and wakes our brains up." Landon
>
> "I like the GoNoodles that make us work out." Nolan

BACKGROUND MUSIC: ENHANCES FOCUS

I have benefited from listening to light classical music while studying. I guarantee that the only reason I passed my ethics class in college was due to my increased focus on unfamiliar topics while music softly played in the background. It was easier to comprehend and then integrate concepts while I listened.

I can also personally attest to the positive effects in the classroom. Depending on the classroom activities taking place, students in my room have had the opportunity to make genre selections for background music. A few years ago, I had a class of vocally talented kids who were excited to be able to add songs to a class playlist. They wrote their school-appropriate selections down (title and performer), and I added them to our list. When we were working independently or in the mornings when they were eating breakfast, we all listened to the student-generated choices. Sometimes, during songs that were very well-liked, you could hear many of them sing softly under their breath. It's one of my favorite memories of that class. If there is no direct instruction going on in our classroom, I can promise there is some genre of light instrumental music playing in the background.

Many academic studies and research support the use of music in classrooms for a variety of reasons (Blackburn 2017, 26–33). Music helps keep the levels of tension and stress to a minimum. Student behaviors are improved as well as an overall sense of wellbeing is established. Musical selections that are played can decrease anxiety in learners, especially during assessments. Distractions are lessened because the students don't hear every little noise from the hallway. Overall, the classroom mood and atmosphere can be positively influenced by subtle background music.

LIGHTS: ENHANCE ATMOSPHERE AND FOCUS

Lighting is used to set the mood for many activities and occasions in everyday life. The classroom is no exception. In the winter, when it's cold outside, we dim the lights for independent reading time, and I find a crackling fireplace video to project on our classroom screen. Everyone grabs a book and settles in immediately to read. People passing by in the hallway wander in and want to read also. The lighting sets the atmosphere perfectly.

In my classroom, lighting is a major influence on the atmosphere of the space. In my opinion, the overhead ceiling lights are too harsh. To overcome the offensive fluorescence, I purchased a set of calming blue filters that cover the ceiling lights. It still seemed like too much light at times. I wanted the atmosphere to be cozier and calmer. So, I added floor lamps, table lamps, and string lights to the decor. Our Student Electrician (remember classroom jobs in Chapter 3?) is in charge of turning all of our lighting options on and then dimming the overhead lights as necessary.

I firmly believe there is a direct correlation between bright lights and loudness. Currently, there are many studies being conducted concerning the best types of lighting for classrooms. Research shows that lighting choices can impact the classroom environment, student performance, and mood (Lekan-Kehinde and Asojo 2021, 371–380). In our classroom, I've noticed the difference in student behavior with overhead lights on versus accent lights. We use the accent lights constantly. The overall atmosphere of the classroom seems calmer, quieter, and more relaxed with them softly glowing around the room. Given the choice, my students will choose accent lights over overhead lights every time.

GUM CHEWING: INCREASES EXECUTIVE FUNCTIONS

I have a penchant for trying out new ideas. I actively seek out concepts that may help my kids relax, focus, or be more comfortable. So when I found an article about the benefits of gum chewing for students, it fit right into my wheelhouse. Research shows that gum chewing can improve mood and spelling acquisition (Wilson, Kim, and Raudenbush 2016, 223–228) and impact standardized test scores in math (Johnston et al. 2012, 455–459).

I have had tons of students who are chewers. They chew on pencils. Pen caps. Ink pens. Straws. The front necklines of their t-shirts. I thought the gum-chewing theory might be the key to stopping the gnawing on other items.

Gum has been a part of my class since the day I read the article. There are guidelines for gum use in order to prevent issues from arising:

► No wrappers should be found on the floor
► All gum is thrown away in the wastebasket
► If you want to chew gum, you bring it yourself
► It has to stay in your mouth
► No popping, smacking, cracking, or blowing bubbles
► No trading gum with others

I completely understand the issues that can get sticky when kids chew gum. There are alternatives if gum doesn't seem like an option you're ready to chew on. For example, plastic straws let kids chew and gnaw without the sticky aftermath of gum. Colored plastic straws can be a viable option that provide the same soothing effects without the mess.

Since we implemented gum or straw chewing, the lifespan of writing materials has definitely increased. The front collars of shirts are dry and unstretched. The kids do seem to concentrate better, and there is not so much idle chatty whispering when they are working independently. The anxiety level of some of the students has decreased. The benefits are wins as far as I am concerned.

FIDGETS: ENHANCE FOCUS

Many teachers visibly blanch at the mention of fidgets. I know. Those spinners are annoying. I agree. However, I do believe that fidgets have truly helped many of my students refocus and concentrate. Therefore, fidget use has developed into a normal part of my classroom, especially since there are many types of fidgets beyond spinners.

Students who have difficulties regulating sensory input can easily become distracted. They seek out sensations to stimulate or calm themselves. Often, their choices are not good for them or for the classroom environment. Fidgets give kids sensory input in a way that is not distracting to their classmates. I've found that fidgets can help improve students' concentration and attention to tasks by allowing the brain to filter out the extra sensory information.

The key to managing fidgets in the classroom, I believe, is creating guidelines for their usage. These are the ones that work for our class:

- ▻ Fidgets are not toys. A fidget is a small object that keeps your hands busy, so you can pay attention and listen better in class.
- ▻ It must be quiet. No one should be distracted by sounds a fidget makes.
- ▻ You should not need to look at the fidget. If you are looking at it too much, you are not paying attention.
- ▻ The fidget needs to stay in your hands or at your spot. Fidgets are not thrown or bounced.

> ▶ Your fidget is for you only. You may not share, trade, or borrow another student's fidget.
> ▶ Fidgets have a purpose: to help you to pay attention in class. Fidgets do not go to specials, lunch, or recess.
> ▶ If the fidget guidelines are not being met, one warning is given. On the next infraction, the fidget goes into your locker for the rest of the day.

The biggest piece of fidget advice that I can offer is this: Do not, not, not decide that, as the teacher, you will buy fidgets for the students to use while working in your classroom. It doesn't work. Trust me on this. I have attempted to purchase fidgets for the room more than once just to find them destroyed, maimed, or picked apart. The kids seem to only take great care of their own fidgets because they don't want anything to happen to them. So, let them bring their fidgets from home.

WEIGHTED NECK SNAKES: REDUCE ANXIETY

Bear with me here. This sounds really odd, so let me explain. Early in my career, I taught "littles"—first graders, to be exact. I had a boy in my class who had a reputation with other teachers. He was introduced to me as "a fart in a skillet" or a "tiny tornado." He and I struggled through a large percentage of our year. Our good days were okay. Our challenging days were unexplainably chaotic.

As the year wrapped up, it came time for track and field day. I could not imagine how I would keep him reined in as we moved from event to event on the track. I was worried that things would spin way out of control in front of parents and the rest of the elementary grades.

The day was overcast and slightly chilly. Parents brought blankets to sit on and cover up with as they watched the events. I had a blanket with me also. My tiny tornado did not, and he was shivering—a lot. I took my heavy blanket, wrapped it around his shoulders, and fashioned it to look like a cape. He immediately settled down, took a seat, and kept the blanket cape on all day.

I was shocked! The weight of the blanket across his shoulders made a huge difference in his behaviors. After our track day experience, I kept a blanket in the classroom for him. If he started to get wound up, all I needed to do was fashion him a blanket cape, and he calmed down. Research supports the use of weighted objects to help students remain calm and still (Buckle, Franzsen, and Bester 2011, 37–41).

Based on the success of the blanket cape, I asked our high school family and consumer science teacher if anyone in her classes would be interested in making a weighted neck/shoulder calming creation. As a project for class, one of my former students sewed two weighted neck tubes for my students. The tubes resembled snakes, so the student sewed eyes on them and added little red forked tongues. My kids voted and selected their names: Jerry and Jenny.

Jerry and Jenny stay in a basket located next to other calming items. Students can decide for themselves if they need Jerry or Jenny based on how they are feeling. Some kids may spend all day with the comfort of the weighted snake across their shoulders; some just need a snake for an hour or so. It's important for the kids to be able to identify how they are feeling and understand what to do to help themselves feel better. Making those autonomous decisions helps them feel more in control of situations that affect them.

Weighted neck snakes make a huge difference for some students.

NOT EVERYTHING WORKS

I've tried a bunch of ideas that sounded really cool and have turned out to be clunkers. Some of the clunkers have been kid-inspired suggestions. Some have been mine.

Blankets in the classroom, for example, was a huge clunker idea. The kids asked if they could bring a blanket or a beach towel to lay on while reading or working independently. They came up with the idea, it didn't seem distracting or counter-pro-ductive, so I obliged.

However, there was no place to store them except for the students' lockers, so everyone was in and out of the room con-stantly. It was incredibly distracting. Whenever students left the room to get or put away their blankets, they had to sign out. That caused an issue for the students who needed to sign out to use the restroom. It was a huge hassle.

The final straw with the blankets came one morning when I heard raised voices in the back of the room. Upon investigation, I found out that one of the girls had gotten a new blanket with some cartoon images. It was a very adult cartoon, not a children's cartoon. The content was definitely not for children. A group of my fifth-grade boys realized it and were causing a ruckus over the blanket. The poor girl had no idea. I settled everyone back down, and after that, all blankets went home, never to return again.

Simple changes make a big difference.

Simple changes make a big difference.

Offering choices in the classroom that allow students to make decisions about their environment directly impacts their learning experience. Having the ability to exert some control over their circumstances is empowering. Students have opportunities to alter their learning environment based on their uniquely ever-changing needs. They begin to understand what helps them focus on their learning and how they work most effectively. The development of those personalized learning insights begins to build a foundation for their future educational pursuits.

ISABELLE: Teachers wear a lot of hats and play such a big role in a kid's development, yet are so underappreciated. What motivates you to keep doing what you're doing?

GINA: I like having the autonomy, the creativity, and the ability to change this or that. I like building those connections with my students. I love it when kids come back down and borrow books or when somebody stops me in the hall and says, "You should read this." Ultimately, I need to have purpose. I need to know that what I'm doing means something. I like to think that with each student I send out into the world, a little piece of me lives on into the future. I like that idea a great deal. I'm not sure that any other career could offer as much long-term satisfaction.

ESTABLISHING RELATIONSHIPS

I'm certain we've all heard the phrase, "Fake it until you make it." There are definitely many occasions when that adage is a worthy strategy. Establishing relationships with your students is not one of those occasions. Kids have a keen sense for spotting insincerity and phoniness. If they don't believe you, then they won't believe in you.

As you peruse the contents, ask yourself,

What am I capable of opening up to?

CHAPTER EIGHT

Making Human Connections with Kids

One morning, a few years ago, I was cruising around the room while buses were arriving and kids were eating breakfast. I noticed one of my boys drawing a Pokémon character in his notebook. Looking a bit closer, I could see the curve of the creature's body and its green color. It was a level 1 Bulbasaur. I could tell because the seed on its back had not evolved yet. (I know my Pokémon characters pretty well. But we'll get to that in a moment!)

I crouched down by this student's chair and complimented his artistic skills. He was blown away! He asked if I played Pokémon GO and what my level was. I gave him a geeky grin, grabbed my phone, and showed him my level 27 status. He was speechless. His level was considerably below mine. I started playing Pokémon GO years ago when it first came out. I liked catching the creatures! I wasn't much of a battler in the gyms, but I had a pretty sizable collection of creatures that elevated the level of my trainer status.

Not too long after our conversation, his mom ran into me. She shared how excited her son was to know that his teacher was a level 27. He was sure he would love fifth grade because he and his teacher were both Pokémon trainers!

Connections like that are priceless.

Discovering that your teacher may have some cool hobbies intrigues kids. One spring afternoon, I stopped by my dad's farm and borrowed the 1962 Impala for the day. It's a beauty: red and black and low to the ground! I pulled in to get gas at a local station. When I walked in to pay and grab a soda, I saw two of my students propped up on their knees in a booth, staring and pointing at the car. With wide, shining eyes and squeaky voices, they yapped about the car's look, the year, and what they would do with one of those.

They called out to me and asked if I had seen it. I smiled, told them I had driven it there, and invited them to go out and see it up close. They whooped and ran out the door, beelining for the car.

Those boys told the story over and over about "Ms. Ruffcorn and her cool classic car that they got to see and sit in." I know because one boy's parents stopped in during conferences to tell me how much the moment meant to her son.

The fact that I had taken the time to show the boys the car and let them sit in it made a positive impression on him because I cared enough to share something I enjoyed with him. I'll bet you have your own stories like this, where a connection blossomed because of shared interests with your students. When students know interesting things about their teachers, it elevates those teachers above the one-dimension person they thought they knew.

What do Pokémon status and classic cars have to do with teaching? Everything.

Relationships are truly the key to everything. That's the bottom line. You could have the most beautifully decorated room, the most perfectly designed lesson, and the most engaging activities. But none of those will work the way they should if you haven't built relationships with your students. Take the time to build genuine relationships with your kids and you will never regret it.

You could have the most beautifully decorated room, the most perfectly designed lesson, and the most engaging activities. But none of those will work the way they should if you haven't built relationships with your students. Take the time to build genuine relationships with your kids and you will never regret it.

INVEST IN STUDENT RELATIONSHIPS

In my experience, the investment of time and effort in building student relationships is worth every minute. You get back what you put in. Kids have to believe in what you say and, most importantly, what you do. You cannot be contradictory. Kids will expect you to act as you say you will. Not doing so will guarantee that you are not the person they hoped you would be.

I always think back to the teachers I wished for when I was in school. What did I need the most when I was a fifth-grade student? Would my fifth-grade self be proud of the teacher I am now?

It's imperative that you let the kids get to know you for them to feel connected to you. Teachers are still sort of mysterious creatures in the minds of most students—especially fifth graders. They know that you're a human being (at least, they're pretty sure of it), but they almost always see you at school. They don't see what you do in your free time. Or how you interact with other non-student human beings. Or if you eat or sleep or talk on the phone or use social media. Students are always surprised to discover information about a teacher's life. Learning that your teacher loves the same foods, watches some of the same shows, and likes to sleep in on the weekends, too, builds a sense of commonality.

Sometimes I eat lunch with my kids. I know that isn't every teacher's idea of how to best spend some of the only planning time that we get. But every once in a while, I enjoy sitting at the long lunch tables and listening to their stories. It brings us closer together. Sharing funny things that happen to us or telling nerdy jokes at lunch is a fabulous way to have some fun and relax a bit. In the lunchroom, I'm not in charge, so I can afford to be a little goofy.

FRIENDLY COMPETITION: ONLINE PRACTICE GAMES

Ever play online classroom practice activities? My class does. I occasionally pop into a game and play alongside the students. It brings a new element to the competition: can we beat the teacher? Now every kid in the room is fully focused. Being able to score more points than the teacher is quite a triumph. Things get intense, and sometimes, you can even feel and hear the energy from outside the classroom. Others are drawn into the room to figure out what's going on.

We were all online playing a game one morning where you choose the right answer and pick a treasure chest. The kids had logged in and started when I decided to surprise them and join in. Choosing the correct root words suddenly became more serious. They giggled every time they bested me and swiped my winnings. We were all laughing and playing as the teacher next door walked in to see what all of the excitement was about. A few minutes later, another teacher stopped in to see what was happening. We had fun, learned the meanings of our root words, and I scored in the top three on the podium. Playing games with your students creates a unique rapport and enforces the concept that learning is fun.

BATHROOM BOX: HONOR STUDENTS' NEEDS

I know every teacher in the world has had a powerful, engaging lesson derailed by students raising their hands to use the restroom. You know what I mean. Everything is happening beautifully. The discussion is amazing. Everyone is eager to participate. Hands are raising and waving. You feel on top of the world. This is fabulous! You call on an excitedly wiggling hand, hoping for another insightful addition to the discourse. Instead, it's a request to use the restroom. The momentum is suddenly brought to a screeching halt because, suddenly, every kid in the room remembers that they also need to use the restroom.

It doesn't have to be that way. In fact, this restroom situation is an opportunity to give students some autonomy. If I, personally, am beginning to feel uncomfortable and I need to use the restroom, I can't concentrate. I quit listening, and all I can think about is needing to go. I am pretty certain that kids feel the same way—or even stronger.

Secondly, if I need to go, I don't want a bunch of attention called to me about it. I know students agree. Older kids hate to be embarrassed about bathroom issues.

Thirdly, I don't want to lose classroom time standing in the hallway while everyone takes a bathroom break together. It takes way too long.

That is how the Bathroom Box came to be. Every morning, as part of their job requirements, the Board Monitor draws a rectangular box in the corner of the board, puts a line down the middle of it, and writes girls on one side and boys on the other. When you need to leave the room, you write your name and draw a line through it, so I know who is out. Upon returning, you erase your name. If someone is on the list below you, that student can leave when you return. Only one boy and one girl can be out at a time. If there is a name under yours when you return, it is not up to you to do anything about it. That person will be in charge of it themselves.

Again, no rocket science involved here either. What is involved is the students' need for autonomy. They are fifth graders. They deserve to be able to independently manage their restroom needs—as adults do. It makes a considerable difference to the kids.

It even showed up on the end-of-the-year survey. When asked, "What did you like the most about fifth grade?" Jayden responded, "Being able to sign out to use the restroom."

HALLWAYS: HUMANIZING STUDENTS

When I walk up a hallway headed to a meeting with other people, we don't walk in a silent single-file line. That would be ridiculous. Everyone in the world walks along with a friend, or a coworker, chatting quietly on the way to their destination. Now, that is normal. Therefore, I strongly believe that's the skill set that my fifth graders need to learn.

I have an aversion to normal classroom hallway management. It's nonsensical. What is it teaching kids? Standing in a straight, single-file line and dutifully walking up the hall in total silence. If I thought that was appealing, I would have become a corrections officer. In fact, I once taught with a lady who should have gone into that occupation. Every foray into the hall was an opportunity for her to threaten, bellow, and screech until her class was deafened into submission. Only once she had exerted her dominance and the line was perfectly straight and silent, could they proceed. Hearing her berate her class made me crazy. Her kids looked embarrassed and miserable. Once they made it to their location, they were generally louder than ever due to their level of hallway frustration.

Instead, each year, I vow to teach my class how to walk up the hall with a partner and talk quietly. As simple as that notion seems, trust me, it's probably one of the most difficult concepts to put into effect. Every time my students leave the classroom, I demonstrate how I control my voice. I'm explicit in what it feels like when you begin to push your voice louder so your partner can hear you. When that feeling begins to happen, everyone needs to be aware of the louder volumes and practice more sound control by lowering their own voices. They may not shush or monitor each other. Everyone is responsible for their own voice level.

We practice every time we travel the halls. Sometimes we start off well and can make it down one hallway before the volume gets out of control. Other times we can only make it partway down one hall. From my position at the end of our line, I can easily hear if the kids have forgotten to keep their voices regulated. When the attempt is unsuccessful, they have to revert back to walking in a single line. The kids have good intentions each time, but making it to the destination with their partners beside them is challenging. Learning impulse control and voice regulation simultaneously is quite an undertaking. Nevertheless, I hold fast to the mantra that every day is a new day, and practice is the only way to learn.

Even if your students are older and you don't walk them to and from different locations, the hallways are still a place to humanize. Be yourself. Let students see the human side of you. Invest a bit of time in genuine conversations. Those interactions are the blocks for building foundations of acceptance, interest, and community with the students.

THE BENEFITS OF HONESTY

Honesty is a major piece of relationship-building with kids, especially those in upper elementary school and beyond. The kids have to be able to trust you. They will never truly open up if they feel you are just not trustworthy. I don't sugarcoat things. It's just not me, which makes me much better suited to teach upper elementary than littles.

My math skills were horrible when I was in school. I share that with my students. As a result, my math grades were not good. I tell them that, too. I tell them that I used to spend almost every recess inside when I was in sixth grade. Why? I didn't know my multiplication tables, and my homework wasn't done before class started. I understand what my frustrated math kids are going through because I remember those feelings when it was my struggle.

Sometimes, your personality and your past can be the most powerful ways of building relationships with your students. When students know their teacher faced the same things that they're facing, it helps. They are not quite getting it, but it helps them understand that they will figure it out. It's not the end of the world, and the proof is that I survived. And so will they.

Reading has always been my thing. I was in the blue bird group in kindergarten. I don't even remember learning to read. I've just been able to do it—that is, until I encountered graphic novels as an adult. I have many graphic novels in my classroom library. My students love them, so I wanted to read them, too. Try as I might, I couldn't figure out how. I was frustrated. It felt like I was missing important details. I didn't seem to comprehend as much as my kids did when they read graphic novels.

Finally, I had to honestly admit to my students that I couldn't read graphic novels. They were eager to offer help. They would take turns sitting with me and explaining how to read using the visual clues and artwork to support the text. They were extremely patient teachers. I grew a fondness for the bright colors and stunning artwork. Eventually, I learned how to access the different types of visual cues to aid in my comprehension.

For me, the graphic novel experience reinforced how students feel when they attempt to tackle a new skill. The kids never thought about the fact that teachers are still learning and growing, too. Plus, my students got another opportunity to share their knowledge with me. The students were in control, helping me build a skill instead of the other way around. Discussing my successes and failures was an integral part of building an honest, authentic learning environment.

APOLOGIZE IF YOU NEED TO

I have mishandled more situations than I can even remember. Guaranteed. Without a doubt. If you are honest with yourself, you know we all do. Things go wrong. Stuff inevitably happens. It happens for all sorts of reasons: a storm front causes barometric pressure to fall, or the moon is full. The list goes on and on. The myriad circumstances that can cause a fissure in your normally easy-going teacher demeanor are limitless. And then you slip. You lose it. You mishandle a situation. It happens.

The way you choose to deal with your reaction can make a huge difference to the relationships you have with your students.

You can't control your circumstances or what happens to you. But you can control how you react.

I choose to apologize. It may be to the whole class. I may apologize to just a student or two. But I always explain myself and genuinely apologize. I'm human, too, and even as an adult, I don't always make a good choice in my behavior. Many kids have never heard an adult admit to being wrong, much less a teacher. It's important that my students know that I don't always make the right choice in dealing with my emotions. It really helps students own their behaviors when they mishandle a situation themselves. Caring about the way you treat others teaches students the value of empathy.

NOW, TRUST YOUR KIDS

Not long ago, I had a rather delicate situation occur that forced me to reassess my thoughts and reactions regarding student behaviors. There was a clutch of boys who would return from various locations in the building, with complaints always seeming to follow them. It ranged from covert whispering to excessive talking to outright arguing with staff members. The first few times, I doled out consequences. After even more complaints, it was time for a talk. I kept the repeat offenders with me instead of sending them to a specials class for an open, honest discussion.

Instead of more punishments, I listened. These boys said they would try to explain themselves to adults, but it was interpreted as disrespectful behavior. Sometimes adults overreact, they said. My kids know that I do not allow disrespect. They also know that they trust me, and, in turn, I trust them to be honest. As they bluntly described different problem situations, they took ownership of their behavior. By the time they were all finished sharing experiences, I was searching for an answer.

I needed a solution that did not undermine anyone else's discipline style but still honored my students. Instead of coming up with the answer on my own, we came to a conclusion unanimously.

 Kids have to feel that you are beside them for guidance, behind them for backup, and ready to catch them when they fall.

Our conclusion? The kids agreed to not say anything at all if they were reprimanded anywhere at school. If they were reprimanded, though, they would talk to me and explain themselves. I agreed not to issue any punitive consequences until I had given them a chance to come to me. Our agreement held for the rest of the year.

The kids learned that as a staff member, I cannot control nor disrespect other adults' decisions. They trusted me enough to know that I would hold up my end of the agreement. I would always listen to their perspective before I made any decisions about consequences.

In order to build genuine relationships with students, they have to believe in the teacher. Kids have to feel that you are beside them for guidance, behind them for backup, and ready to catch them when they fall. If students don't feel connected to you, if they don't feel like you've "got them," they don't buy in to anything.

Relationships are the key element to everything. If you establish a solid foundation, you have what you need for successful learners to develop in a successful classroom.

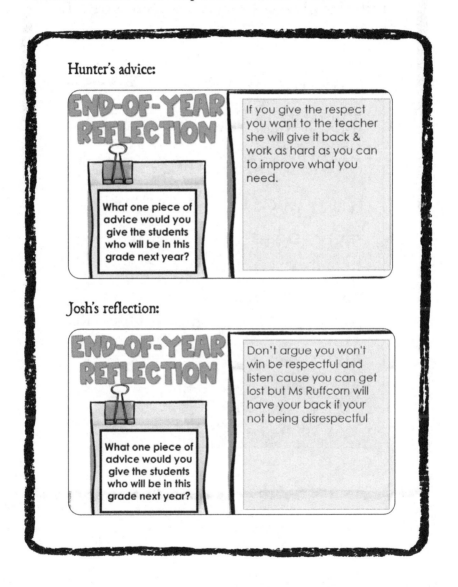

In our end-of-the-year survey, I asked, "What should every teacher know, have, or do in order to be a good teacher?" The anonymous reply was, "They need to get us."

Ms. Ruffcorn,
Thank you for teaching
me all I know. It was a thrill
having you as my teacher.
Your belief in me makes me
belive in myself. Thanks for
being with me. If I scoreing you
from one to ten, I wold give
you a ten! I had a wonderful
year! I was great.
Love Rachael

ISABELLE: What are some things you've learned about yourself as you've developed your style of teaching?

GINA: I learned that educationally, I was lucky. I never understood how much I took for granted. Once when I was struggling over why certain steps needed to be done in a lesson for a class I was taking, an instructor asked me, "How did you learn how to read?" I had no recollection. My response was, "I don't know, I've always just known how to read." And she explained, "That's because you've never had to work at it." For people who did have it work at acquiring those skills, it's a huge issue. If you don't ever have it happen to you, you don't understand. I had never encountered any of those issues when I was a student. As I developed my teaching style, I needed to address all of the possibilities of things that might help make the workings a little easier for others.

CHAPTER NINE

Behavior Expectations

Fifth grade was my favorite year when I was a kid. I remember loving everything about it (except for math). I had the cool male teacher for my homeroom. I discovered an amazing book, *A Wrinkle in Time*. It made such an impact on me that I wrote a play about it for a book report project and got an A. We decorated our lockers with all sorts of cool posters and quotes that we thought made us seem grown up. Fifth graders ruled the playground because we were the oldest grade in the building. It was an epic year, even if I did have to get braces.

I've taught other grades before, and those were okay. But, there is no grade I would rather teach than fifth. They are still young enough to be funny and silly. And they are old enough that I feel like I'm making a lasting impact on their personal development as they grow. You may teach older or younger students than mine, and I'll bet you have reasons why they're unique and special. I hope you do. To me, though, fifth graders are the best.

SETTING HIGH EXPECTATIONS

Due to my fond memories of fifth grade, I feel compelled to give my kids a similar experience. I want their year to be one that they remember with a smile when they think back on it.

I have pretty high expectations for my students. Those behavioral expectations are non-negotiable in our classroom. In fact, they are probably the only part of our classroom that I decide on unilaterally. They've been solidly steadfast since I began teaching. Leadership, personal accountability, and kindness are all qualities that I value. With support, guidance, and practice, students will learn to rise to the level of expectations that have been set.

I know some people think it's hard enough to teach the standards, let alone all of the "other stuff." I get it. There are a ton of duties and responsibilities placed on teachers. I know. Hear me out on this one. This is my theory:

I am just one of many teachers that a student will have. I'm not the only one who will teach a concept to a kid. There are a plethora of talented teachers still to come into their lives. Students will be exposed to curricular areas and the aligned standards a lot. However, fifth grade only happens once. The kids are only ten years old at one time in their lives. I am the only teacher they will have at ten years old in fifth grade. I'm the person to teach the important skills for developing positive behaviors at this stage of their lives. No, it's not in my contract to teach the "other stuff," but my teacher's gut tells me it's the right thing to do for my kids. No matter what you teach, I hope you also have your own lessons and legacies you want your students to experience and remember fondly.

OPENINGS FOR LEADERSHIP EXPERIENCES

Since fifth grade is the highest grade in the elementary end of my building, fifth graders should be role models. They should be the leaders. I expect my students to set a good example of how to behave for the younger students.

I jump on every chance I can find to give my students leadership opportunities. Some examples:

- ► If I hear something in the daily announcements that my class can assist with, I volunteer them.
- ► If I'm in the office grabbing my mail and another teacher mentions needing help with her younger kids' shoe tying abilities, my kids can help out.
- ► When the kindergarteners are learning sight words, my class would love to be flashcard buddies. Making connections with the younger grades makes our school community stronger.
- ► If I know I am going to be gone, I appoint two of my students to be the classroom leaders for the substitute.
- ► When I have lunch duty, the fifth graders select a younger buddy to walk back from the cafeteria with. They model proper hallway behavior for the younger kids.

► During the rollerskating unit in Physical Education class, my fifth graders help out with the kindergarten classes until the littles can skate on their own. When younger students interact like this with the fifth graders, it empowers their own developing leadership skills.

After my students have a few leadership experiences, many will step up individually to assist others. The compliments and positive reactions reinforce the importance of leadership behaviors in the fifth graders.

PERSONAL RESPONSIBILITY OR PERSONAL ACCOUNTABILITY

This one can be difficult to instill in kids. Oftentimes, students are praised for tattling on their classmates. The tattletale-type behavior can be hard to overcome for some students. Kids calling out each other's inappropriate behavior compounds the issue. Inevitably, students feel it is their job to let the teacher know that someone is doing something they shouldn't. The question I consistently ask is simple: "Who are you in charge of?" The expectation is that kids are only in charge of themselves. It's not up to anyone to monitor or micromanage anyone else. Each student is in charge of their own behavior and decisions. Everyone monitors themselves. Taking responsibility for their own actions helps tremendously when an issue arises. Kids can't say that it wasn't their fault. They are held completely accountable because they are in charge of themselves.

KINDNESS MATTERS

Requiring everyone to treat each other kindly is a huge expectation. Students don't have to like, agree with, or believe in things that others do. Everyone has to be kind to each other. There is no other option. That is the expectation for everyone, including me. Just like everything else that kids are trying to learn, showing kindness to others isn't always easy. The biggest infringements on the kindness expectation are things that kids will try to explain away as teasing or joking. When one student comes to me to discuss how unkind another student was to them, we have a talk. The defining question is, "Did the person you were talking about laugh?" If not, then it wasn't funny to them. That's unkind. Genuine apologies need to be made, and the parties involved need to tell me what they have learned and what they can do to make sure it doesn't happen again.

EMPHASIZE KINDNESS

During large group read-alouds, I select audiobooks that reinforce the expectation of kindness. These novels contain situations that kids routinely experience. It helps students to identify how unkind actions affect others. Pausing the novel to discuss how characters are feeling and acting toward each other lets the kids share their understanding of kindness.

The two novels that I rely on the most to reinforce kindness are *Wonder* by Patricia Palacio and *Out of My Mind* by Sharon Draper. Both novels are incredibly powerful and speak directly to the age group of my students. Their themes of friendship, empathy, and kindness allow for many extension activities.

After finishing *Wonder*, the whole class takes a vow of friendship based on the message of "always choosing kind."

The most powerful kindness and empathy activity that I've experienced as a teacher occurred during our *Out of My Mind* read-aloud. The main character uses a non-electronic talking board as her only means of communication, so I printed off copies of talking boards for my students. They were prepared to point to or spell out information using the talking board for all of their interactions during lunch and recess. Once they all came back to the classroom, everyone was ready to talk about their experiences. The students explained how difficult it was to talk to friends without using words. They shared feelings of frustration and futility. Kids had a better understanding of how hard it would be to make friends without being able to speak. They became much more sensitive and patient when they interacted with other students.

EXPECTATIONS, NOT RULES

I was not a kid with discipline problems when I was in school. From kindergarten all the way through my senior year, I never had even one detention or negative office call to my parents. In fact, during my eighth-grade year, I scored extremely high in my percentile rank on my state assessments and was made assistant principal for the day. I've always been a learner. It's what I do best. Nevertheless, the word *rules* has always bothered me. Instantly I find myself bristling a bit. I've never reacted well to the concept of adhering to rules, especially those that seem arbitrary. I prefer expectations rather than rules. It may be a matter of semantics, but in my opinion, expectations are set to be achievable. Rules are just restrictions.

I don't want the first few days of a bright, shiny new school year to be quashed by the issuance of a litany of rules. So, I choose to set expectations for my students. Setting expectations affects the mood of the classroom environment in a more positive manner. Growing, changing, and becoming more aware of their behavioral choices is more important to me than knowing about and not breaking a set of rules.

WHAT TO FOCUS ON?

When choosing behavior expectations, it's essential to decide what you really want the students to strive toward. My selections developed over time based on my observations—what I heard kids say and what I watched them struggle with. The expectations that I focus on are areas that I believe are meaningful for the developmental stage of my students. The skills they learn will be beneficial to their continued success as learners. You know your students, and you know how they can grow as human beings. Let your experience and your observations be your guide.

When it comes to explaining behavior expectations, it's imperative to be succinct. Extra verbosity can cloud the understanding students need to have in order for the expectations to be met. The behavior changes students work toward attaining require more attention and focus. Steadily and consistently requiring expectations to be met is key. That is definitely easier to accomplish if the number of expectations is manageable. In order for kids to internalize and begin to apply the concepts, expectations have to be firmly established and attainable.

WHEN THINGS DON'T WORK

Even though expectations are firmly in place, kids are kids. Sometimes, altering the behaviors required to meet the expectations is hard. It's easier to fall back into making the wrong choices. Impulses override. The teacher's response is critical.

Empathy is the best and most significant teacher response. It's hard for kids to keep everything together and meet behavior expectations for themselves. I share small stories of how often I've let my impulses have too much control and how poorly that has affected my behavioral choices. I goof up, too, even as an adult. I was walking down a long hall at school one afternoon many years ago. It had rained outside, and I discovered that my shoes make this kinda cool squeaky noise. Impulsivity overrode. I started happily squeaking down the hall, making rhythms and adjusting volumes. My principal charged around the corner, ready to reprimand a student for all that squeaking. Instead, he found me. It was an inappropriate behavior choice on my part driven by an impulse that I didn't control. Students shouldn't think that they are the only people who make the wrong choices sometimes. They need to know that growth and change do not happen all at once just because behavior expectations are in place. Everyone deserves chances to continue to work toward making better, more responsible decisions. There is always a new day and a new opportunity to try again.

THE IMPACT OF EXPECTATIONS

I genuinely hope that I am able to make an impact on the lives of my students by setting expectations and working toward achieving them. I want to feel like my students are better leaders, kinder people, and more responsible young adults after their year with me. I hope we all feel that way. With every student I teach, a part of me goes with them into their future as they continue setting and meeting expectations for themselves.

With every student I teach, a part of me goes with them into their future as they continue setting and meeting expectations for themselves.

ISABELLE: I'm sure that with such a unique teaching style comes its own set of unique challenges. What are some things related to your teaching style that you still struggle with today?

GINA: There are times when I would like to just run everything myself. There are times where it would save some time, some stress, where it would be easier to be a controlling dictator. There are times where I have to sit back and take a deep breath and think, " there's a reason why choice and autonomy are necessary, there's a reason why we're all in this together." There are moments where I find myself having to stop and count to ten because it would be a lot easier to say, "Here, just give me that, and I will do it." I would say that if there was anything that I still haven't managed to completely conquer, it would be those frustrational moments.

CHAPTER TEN

Supporting Each Other

I was driving to a teacher conference with a pair of teacher friends from another part of the country. It was early morning and, as teachers do, we were talking about, well, you know... teaching. Comments. Jokes. Laughing until everyone in the car had tears streaming down their faces. As we caught our breath, one of my friends said, "I sure do wish you were my kid's teacher. But that wouldn't ever be possible. With your hair and your tattoos, you'd never get hired."

I was taken aback. I stopped. I looked at my friends and asked, "Where do your pink-haired kids go? Who do those kids identify with? Who is their person?"

Neither of them had an answer. I shared my thoughts about abolishing the nonsensical belief that tattoos and "unnatural" hair color are deviant, flaky, or unprofessional. "In my school," I explained, "the kids with funky colored hair and unique styles are generally drawn to me. When I have recess duty, or I'm in the halls, those kids identify with me almost instantly."

See, I joyously celebrate my individuality. In turn, my students feel more welcome and accepted for expressing their own individualities. I know the "off the beaten path" kids. I am the person they see daily and identify with.

That car conversation has stayed with me for years. It probably always will. The concept of being unhirable based on hair color or tattoos seems incredibly judgmental, especially in the field of education. I'm pretty sure that my intellect, abilities, and integrity are not subject to change due to whatever color my hair happens to be on any given day or whether or not I decide on another tattoo.

Be unabashedly yourself, and let your students know who you are. Grow, nurture and develop independent, empathetic, compassionate, understanding, kind students. Teach them the futility of preconceived notions.

As you build relationships with your students, appropriately share what you value and what you believe in. Show your kids that their individuality is celebrated by celebrating your own. Be unabashedly yourself, and let your students know who you are. Grow, nurture and develop independent, empathetic, compassionate, understanding, kind students. Teach them the futility of preconceived notions.

If someone's appearance is more distracting or important than your lesson- What are you teaching & how engaging is it? @gruffcorn13

Hair color and tattoos don't affect a person's ability to teach.

NO MORE BEING A BYSTANDER

I have always been a huge supporter of the kids who walk to the beat of a different drum. Oftentimes, those are the students who are most affected by teasing, rudeness, and unkind behaviors. I firmly believe that all people should be allowed to express themselves and their individuality without fear of being ridiculed for being different.

I will regretfully admit that, in the past, I left the anti-bullying lessons to the guidance counselor. I thought I was doing enough to prevent bullying by reinforcing our school policy and monitoring the hallway outside my room.

I was wrong.

I discovered just how wrong I was one afternoon when a distraught student appeared in my doorway. He was incredibly upset and wanted to talk to me about how unkind some of his classmates were to him. As he poured out his story to me, I felt sad. I was sad for him and sad for all of the other kids that were going through similar situations. I really hadn't done anything to alleviate the bullying problem at all. Just because I hadn't seen any overt examples, I assumed that everything was okay.

It wasn't okay, even though I never saw anything. That's the way that bullies work. Rarely do they ever do anything when adults are around. I needed to empower my students to act on their own. They were the ones who were there when the bullying situations arose. They were the ones who needed the skills to understand how to stop being bystanders.

I searched for authentic examples of real situations that students faced. This would be the best way to launch into honest discussions. In those discussions, the students could hear each other's thoughts and feelings. If they knew that other classmates agreed that the mean behaviors needed to stop, it might empower them to step up and speak out. I found resources that mirrored situations that would be easily identifiable for the students.

It was time for action. I incorporated a new piece to our morning meetings once a week. I called it "Monday Motivation." Every Monday morning, we watched realistic school videos that focused on different types of unkind behaviors. I specifically targeted videos that showed genuine situations reinforcing the concept of being the person to speak up if someone was being teased, bullied, or mistreated. We discussed each scenario. We concentrated on honesty and ownership of our own behaviors. The kids seemed surprised to discover that most of them were taking part in these unkind situations due to their silence.

They were astonished that not doing anything was just as bad as being the bully. They thought if they were ignoring the unkind person's behavior, then it would stop.

I refused to accept shallow responses from the kids. Students have been taking part in lessons about bullying in school for years. I'd been there for many guidance lessons, and I knew what sort of basic responses students gave. When asked, they would regurgitate the typical responses. That allowed them to escape without truly examining their own thoughts and actions. When the situations occurred in their own lives, they did nothing. I was committed to digging deeper. In order to get the kids to answer honestly, I would have to prod a bit. The kids needed to acknowledge and own their behaviors. In an earlier chapter, I shared that students can spot phony behavior from their teacher in an instant. Students demand fairness and authenticity. If that's the case, they should expect it in a hard discussion like this about their own behavior. I knew what I saw happening. They knew exactly what their roles had been in many unkind situations.

I figured that if I were as straightforward and candid as possible, that would get us started. I openly shared personal experiences from my childhood on both sides of the issue. There were times when I was a snotty, unkind beast at recess. I wasn't proud of myself, but I owned my actions. There were other times when kids were awful to me because I had thick glasses and braces. I stressed the fact that most situations can be diffused by at least one person. I needed the students to be honest with themselves in order to make a shift in their behaviors. They had to feel empowered to stand up for each other. Just being bystanders wouldn't cut it.

All of these conversations about standing up for each other built autonomy in my students. They helped them to make the right decisions—on their own—when they needed to. The more they trusted their own feelings of self-reliance and determination, the easier it would be to diffuse situations. I wanted them to be strong enough to make positive changes in the way everyone was treated. Personal responsibility, leadership, and kindness are all components of self-regulation, self-determination, and self-sufficiency. Students need opportunities to practice these skills. When they do, they'll be the ones to stop the bullying, not a curriculum pushed by the school.

DOING MORE TO CONNECT

I'm not afraid to talk about my missteps. As I mentioned above, I've missed the signs that students were treating each other poorly. But I have also missed situations happening inside my students over the years that I should have noticed. Kids reacted oddly, and I wondered if there was something more going on. Atypical behaviors arose from students, and I didn't get to the root of the problem despite my best intentions or efforts.

I genuinely regret not doing more for the kids whose cues I missed.

I question myself as I reflect on circumstances and events. Am I noticing the nuances of my students' personalities? Am I in tune with my students enough that if something were really wrong, I'd be able to recognize their need? Those thoughts keep me aware of the importance of being connected to my students.

CHECKING IN WITH STUDENTS

I have increased the focus on my student's social and emotional needs. I've tried lots of different ways to check in with them. I'd love to find enough time to sit with and authentically talk to all of them consistently. But it's impossible.

Teachers often use tech to check in with students. Kids can easily record responses on websites geared toward tracking their daily emotions. But many platforms have canned, one-size-fits-all content. My students aren't one-size-fits-all kids. They quickly lose interest. The sites we used also lacked the ability to notify me if a student was having a concern that warranted my prompt attention.

What's the solution? For me, it was a combination. I decided to use online personalized questions with a response system to easily access answers, and time to sit down with kids. I settled on using Google Forms for student check-ins. (If you're a Microsoft school, Microsoft Forms works just as well.) I hunted all over teacher groups and sites to harvest styles, questions, and other information.

I explained the "why" to my students. What was happening in their lives and what they were going through was important to me. I wanted to be responsive. So we launched a daily check-in process. I quickly learned that daily was too much for me and for the kids too. We talked about setting up a new schedule for check-ins that would not be as busy. Together as a class, we chose Monday and Thursday as our days. Why? Monday started our week. Thursday was our mid-week point.

The students liked the personalized feel of the check-ins and the ability to share things with me. They also seemed to be fond of the fact that I truly wanted their thoughts, opinions, and reactions. I liked the ability to create different kinds of questions and tailor them to our class.

CRAFTING A STUDENT CHECK-IN

I begin the check-in with a greeting and a picture. I usually always use my Bitmoji avatar—a cartoon version of myself. The kids think my avatar is funny. I make sure to include a feel-good sentence or two that is inviting and welcoming. The check-ins only contain four or five questions. The first two questions are always "choose your today feeling" and "explain why you chose that feeling." I consistently end the form with a wish or a hope for our day and another silly avatar picture.

What did you do well last week? *

Long answer text

What can you improve on this week? *

Long answer text

Is there anything you want to share with me? Do you have any questions I can help with? *

Long answer text

Students respond to these digital check-ins regularly.

Are there any questions you have that I can answer for you? *

Long answer text

Is there anything I can do to help make you week a great one? *

Long answer text

I'm glad you are all here!

I like to end my check-ins with a fun Bitmoji image.

Here are the questions that have given me the most helpful insights:

- ► How are you feeling today?
- ► Please explain why you chose your feeling answer.
- ► What is something that you are grateful for today?
- ► What is something that puts a smile on your face?
- ► Name one adult at school who you trust and could talk to if you needed to.

- Is there anything you want or need to share with me about how things are going in your life?
- Do you have any questions I can help with?
- Tell me one exciting thing that happened this week— something fun, an achievement, a goal reached.
- Tell one not-so-great thing that happened—something that upset you, a disagreement you had.
- Finish this sentence: I wish my teacher knew . . .
- Do you look forward to coming to school? Why or why not?
- What would make school a better place for you?
- What do you want me to know about you?

RESPONDING TO STUDENT CHECK-INS

The check-ins are part of our early routine before we begin our morning meeting. I make a habit of quickly looking through the students' replies as they submit them. Any reactions that require attention can be attended to right away before the day takes off.

Based on responses from the students, I felt more connected with their thoughts, feelings, and opinions. If there was an event they were excited about, I knew about it. When they shared information about themselves, I was able to learn more about them. If there was an issue, I could offer help in order to diffuse the situation. I was able to find time during our day to sit and talk individually with specific students based on the check-in forms.

I've gained a greater awareness of my students' mindsets. Additionally, I understood their motivations and behaviors more clearly. If I read that a kid was tired, didn't sleep last night, fought with a parent, and was upset, then I considered those elements as the student struggled with settling into our routines. So we spent some quiet time and just chatted. Without the check-in information, I would have missed or completely compounded the underlying issues.

I'll chat with students about topics from the check-in forms. I'll follow up with questions based on their replies. This proves to the students that I am reading and interested in their answers. My increased attention spurs the kids' buy-in. Soon, they eagerly strike up conversations with me about a variety of topics. Since student input is highly encouraged and valued in our class, the kids begin to suggest subjects and questions for the check-in forms. As more time passes, the kids realize that I take their answers seriously and pay attention to what they share. They feel cared for and valued. Then, their replies become more candid. They open up more. Once, I learned that one of my kids was having an issue with terrifying night-mares that made them unable to get a decent night's sleep. With their permission, I spoke with the guidance counselor. The counselor met with my student and then later with their parents. With a circle of caring people working together, even-tually, the child's nightmares began to lessen, and sleep came more easily.

One thing I wish my teacher knew about is.......

I don't like razing my hand because I think I have it but if i don't get it I feel dum

1 response

Sometimes when I'm lonely this class makes me feel like I'm not alone.

1 response

EVERYONE SUPPORTS EVERYONE: STUDENTS AND TEACHER

Encouraging students to stand up for each other and regular student check-ins have both been powerful in our classroom. They've helped the students support each other. Plus, they've helped me to support them in ways only a teacher should. They've built stronger connections between my kids and me. Our sense of community heightened. I've never regretted taking time with students to reinforce skills that will help them develop into empathetic, responsible, adaptable, confident learners. Reading through the student feedback at the end of our year, I hoped the thoughts they shared would stick with them.

The advice they left for the next class of fifth graders gave me renewed faith:

"Be yourself." Sean

"You need to be yourself." Jason

"And to get along. That means no name calling, no bullying and no trying to beat each other up." Chloe

"They need to be respectful to each other. They also need to make good choices." Nolan

"They need to know how to get along." Rylan

"They should always listen to each other and be nice." Mickenna

ISABELLE: What about giving kids autonomy is so important to you that it stops you from just running everything yourself or in a more "traditional" way?

GINA: It's the fact that if you don't ever give kids any choices, how will they know how to make them? I think adults in general spend a lot of time saying to kids, "You need to make better choices" or "Did you think about what you were doing?" or "Why would you have done that?" and I think why would they not have done that? How do they know 'how to' do things if you don't ever give them any autonomy? I don't know where you're supposed to pick that skill up at. Everything is a learning experience; there are some kids that it's going to come to easily and there are others who are going to struggle a little bit more. If kids never get any experiences at all, how are we ever going to expect them to understand how to make a good choice? These are small decisions now, but soon, some of those decisions won't be. Eventually you'll be running up against some large life decisions that are really going to affect what happens to you, and to your future. If you never had a chance to practice making any decisions, and then the big ones start to come at you, I'm not sure what your success rate is.

CONCLUSION

I was supposed to be a nurse. I've wanted to be a nurse ever since I attended a career fair in junior high. I was working in a hospital and attending nursing classes. Everything was progressing nicely.

Then, I volunteered in my daughter's kindergarten class. Everything changed.

One day, I heard myself saying to a friend, "You know, maybe I think I want to teach."

The more I thought about teaching, the more it continued to feel right. I applied to a teaching program, jumped in with both feet, and never looked back.

I am still teaching in the same school where I student-taught nineteen years ago. But I am not the same teacher. From first grade to sixth grade to reading recovery to middle school to high school credit recovery, I've seen a lot. I've learned some unique lessons. My experiences have transformed me into the teacher I am today. And it's shown me some important things about schools that I hope resonate with everyone:

➤ A bad experience at school can be emotionally debilitating for a student.

- ▶ Socioeconomic status and poverty play a huge role in a family's educational support system.
- ▶ Students—especially those with diverse psychosocial needs in nontraditional educational settings—need a multitude of different learning strategies.
- ▶ Building relationships with students is key to everything.

In some ways, students require different offerings and opportunities than they have been given in the past. The world is asking more of them. They need opportunities to become leaders, to stand up, to speak up, to be kind, and to take the responsibility of their future into their own hands. In that way, they need a different kind of educational experience. Their teachers and their classrooms must reflect those needs.

But in many ways, they also need the same things that students have always needed. They want to know that someone believes in them. They must know that yes, they can do many things they never dreamed of doing. They are capable when they work on their own, and they are capable when they team up with others.

Students deserve a classroom that sets them up for success—not just success on standardized tests and report cards, but success in life. The classroom can prepare them to collaborate with co-workers, to have successful partnerships, to do work that matters, and to set high goals that they can accomplish.

Students gain confidence when they're in a classroom like that. They understand that they belong. They see how bright their future is. They know that they have a voice and a choice, and they see how powerful that is.

The bottom line is this: at the end of every day, the only thing that truly matters is the relationships you build with students. The way they feel, the choices they have, the decisions they learn to make for themselves all connect the kids to the teacher. Those pieces can't be quantitatively measured, yet they mean more than any data ever collected.

Educators are drawn, or more specifically, *called* to the teaching profession to establish connections with students. Why? Because they understand that the future of our world depends on the relationships and understanding children gain from a myriad of compelling, engaging experiences. Our classrooms are manifestations of us as teachers. They embody what we believe in. The way we design them and the methods we use to manage them are based on our own personal mindsets.

Don't let other people's opinions or perceptions of what a classroom should look like intimidate you into not making changes in your room as you forge those vital relationships with your students.

Don't become overwhelmed by all of the educational expectations. The task of balancing testing results, student rankings, and percentages gained toward mastery weighs heavily against fostering emotional growth, empathy, compassion, understanding, creativity, and kindness. It's vital to remember the real reason teachers teach. Don't lose focus.

Be honest. Add some humor. All life experience lessons don't have to be bleak and tenuous.

And whenever possible, no matter what it is, put it in the hands of the students. They are our future. They have a voice—and a strong one. They have the power to make this world what we envision it to be.

They see it. We can do this together.

Our class. Our voice.

MORE RESOURCES

For more resources to help you bring autonomy and voice to the students in your classroom, go to GinaRuffcorn.com

REFERENCES

Blackburn, Heather. 2017. "Music in the Classroom." *International Journal of the Whole Child* 2, no. 1 (April): 26–33.

Buckle, Fransli, Denise Franzsen, and Juanita Bester. 2011. "The effect of the wearing of weighted vests on the sensory behaviour of learners diagnosed with attention deficit hyperactivity disorder within a school context." *South African Journal of Occupational Therapy* 41, no. 3 (December): 37–41.

Johnston, Craig A., Chermaine Tyler, Sandra A. Stansberry, Jennette P. Moreno, and John P. Foreyt. 2012. "Brief report: Gum chewing affects standardized math scores in adolescents." *Journal of Adolescence* 35, no. 2 (April): 455–459.

Lekan-Kehinde, Michael, and Abimbola Asojo. 2021. "Impact of Lighting on Children's Learning Environment: A Literature Review." *WIT Transactions on Ecology and the Environment* 253: 371–380.

Wilson, Andrew, Wonsun Kim, and Bryan Raudenbush. 2016. "The Effects of Chewing Cinnamon Flavored Gum on Mood, Feeling and Spelling Acquisition." *English Language Teaching* 9 no. 6: 223–228.

ACKNOWLEDGEMENTS

The first thank you I need to bestow is to my friend, colleague, and editor, Matt Miller. From the morning I sent a text saying, "I think I am ready to write my book," you believed in me, encouraged me, and guided me. I cannot imagine trusting my teacher's heart and soul to anyone other than you.

My husband, Mark, deserves huge piles of kudos for supporting me through the entire writing experience. Your pride in me utterly overwhelms me. Thank you for making things "not things" and for loving me.

Thank you, Mike Soskil, for doing me a great honor. You and I go back to the very beginning. Having you remember a conversation we had about this book's conception many, many years ago brought tears to my eyes.

ABOUT THE AUTHOR

Gina Ruffcorn is in her nineteenth year of teaching at West Harrison Community School in Mondamin, Iowa. Over the years, she taught high school credit recovery, middle school, reading recovery, first grade, and sixth grade before she found her forever home in fifth grade. She has been the one and only fifth-grade teacher in the district for thirteen years and counting.

Gina has a bachelor's degree from Buena Vista University in Storm Lake, Iowa, and a master's degree in literacy and twenty-first century technologies from the University of Nebraska in Omaha.

Gina was one of the original founding members of Skype Master Teachers. She spent seven years as a Microsoft Innovative Educator Expert and a Global Learning Mentor. Currently, she is a GoNoodle Ambassador, a Kahoot Ambassador, and a Kahoot Verified Educator.

In her spare time, Gina likes to yak on the phone with her daughter, Miranda, ride motorcycles with her husband, Mark, and watch bad reality T.V. with her two cats, Vivian and Dennis.

She can be easily reached in the Twitterverse @gruffcorn13.

Made in the USA
Coppell, TX
01 July 2022

79433557R00096